THE ELDER SCROLLS V: SKYRIM®
THE SKYRIM® LIBRARY, VOLUME III: THE ARCANE

ISBN: 9781783293216

Published by Titan Books,
A division of Titan Publishing Group Ltd.,
144 Southwark St., London, SE1 0UP, United Kingdom

Special thanks to Steve Perkins, Mike Kochis, and Paris Nourmohammadi with Bethesda Softworks,
and Todd Howard with Bethesda Game Studios.

www.elderscrolls.com
www.bethsoft.com

A CIP catalogue record for this title is available from the British Library.
First edition: September 2016

10 9 8 7 6 5 4 3

Printed in China.

To receive advance information, news, competitions and exclusive offers online, please sign up for
the Titan newsletter on our website: www.titanbooks.com

What did you think of this book? We love to hear from our readers. Please email us at:
readerfeedback@titanemail.com, or write to us at the above address.

THE SKYRIM LIBRARY

VOLUME III
THE ARCANE

TITAN BOOKS

Contents

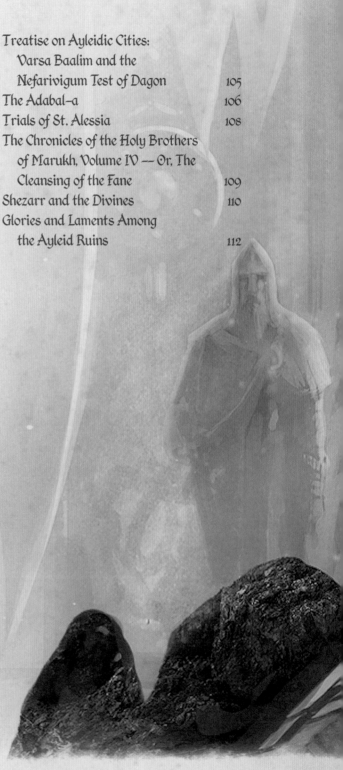

Magicka

Arcana Restored: A Handbook	8
The Charwich-Koniinge Letters	10
On the Great Collapse	24
The Apprentice's Assistant	25
The Final Lesson	27
Feyfolken	30
The Cake and The Diamond	42
Fragment: On Artaeum	45
The Old Ways	47
An Accounting of the Elder Scrolls	49
Effects of the Elder Scrolls	51
N'Gasta! Kvata! Kvakis!	53
Souls, Black and White	54
The Book of Life and Service	55

Religion

The Monomyth	56
A Children's Anuad: The Paraphrased	65
An Overview of Gods and Worship in Tamriel	67
Varieties of Faith in the Empire	69
Lives of the Saints	81
The Doors of the Spirit	83
Spirit of Nirn	84
The Talos Mistake	85
Pension of the Ancestor Moth	87
The Reclamations: The Fall of the Tribunal and the Rise of the New Temple	88
Nchunak's Fire and Faith	92
A Dream of Sovngarde	93
Sovngarde: A Reexamination	95
The Amulet of Kings	99
The Last King of the Ayleids	101
Magic from the Sky	103
Treatise on Ayleidic Cities: Varsa Baalim and the Nefarivigum Test of Dagon	105
The Adabal-a	106
Trials of St. Alessia	108
The Chronicles of the Holy Brothers of Marukh, Volume IV — Or, The Cleansing of the Fane	109
Shezarr and the Divines	110
Glories and Laments Among the Ayleid Ruins	112

2920: The Last Year of the First Era

Morning Star 114
Sun's Dawn 119
First Seed 123
Rain's Hand 128
Second Seed 133
Mid Year 138
Sun's Height 143
Last Seed 148
Hearth Fire 155
Frostfall 160
Sun's Dusk 167
Evening Star 173

Aedra and Daedra

Aedra and Daedra 180
The Book of Daedra 181
The Daedric Artifact Book 186
Darkest Darkness 190
Varieties of Daedra 192
Spirit of the Daedra 195
Invocation of Azura 197
Azura and the Box 199
The Anticipations 201
Beggar Prince 202
Changed Ones 204
Wabbajack 205
The Woodcutter's Wife 206
The Cabin in the Woods 208
The House of Troubles 212
Opusculus Lamae Bal ta Mezzamortie:
    A Brief Account of Lamae Bal and
    the Restless Death 213
Amongst the Draugr 214
Sixteen Accords of Madness 218

Arcana Restored: A Handbook

by Wapna Neustra Praceptor Emeritus

FORM THE FIRST: Makest thou the Mana Fountain to be Primed with Pure Gold, for from Pure Gold only may the Humors be rectified, and the Pure Principles coaxed from the chaos of Pure Power. Droppest thou then the Pure Gold upon the surface of the Mana Fountain. Takest thou exceeding great care to safeguard yourself from the insalubrious tempests of the Mana Fountain, for through such Assaults may one's health be utterly Blighted.

FORM THE SECOND: Make sure that thou havest with you this Excellent Manual, so that thou might speak the necessary Words straightaway, and without error, so that thou not in carelessness cause thyself and much else to discorporate and disorder the World with your component humors.

FORM THE THIRD: Take in hand the item to be Restored, and hold it forth within the Primed Fountain, murmuring all the while the appropriate phrases, which are to be learned most expeditiously and faultlessly from this Manual, and this Manual alone, notwithstanding the vile calumnies of Kharneson and Rattor, whose bowels are consumed by envy of my great learning, and who do falsely give testament to the efficacies of their own Manuals, which are in every way inferior and steeped in error.

FORM THE FOURTH: Proceed instantly to Heal thyself of all injuries, or to avail yourself of the Healing powers of the Temples and Healers, for though the agonies of manacaust must be borne by any who would Restore a prized Arcana to full Potency, yet it is not wise that suffering be endured unduly, nor does the suffering in any way render the Potency more Sublime, notwithstanding the foolish speculations of Kharneson and Rattor, whose faults and wickednesses are manifest even to the least learned of critics.

The Charwich-Koniinge Letters

Book I

6 Suns Height, 3E 411. Kambria, High Rock.

My Dear Koniinge,

I hope this letter reaches you in Sadrith Mora. It's been many weeks since I've heard from you, and I hope that the address that I have for you is still up-to-date. I gave the courier some extra gold, so if he doesn't find you, he is to make inquiries to your

whereabouts. As you can see, after a rather tedious crossing, I've at long last made my way from Bhoriane to my favorite principality in High Rock, surprisingly literate and always fascinating Kambria. I at once ensconced myself in one of the better libraries here, becoming reacquainted with the locals and the lore. At the risk of being overly optimistic, I think I might have struck on something very interesting about this mysterious fellow, Hadwaf Neithwyr.

Many here in town remember him, though few very fondly. When Hadwaf Neithwyr left, so too did a great plague. No one thinks it a coincidence.

According to my contacts here, Azura is not his only master. It may be that when he summoned forth the Daedra and accepted her Star, he was doing so for someone named Baliasir. Apparently, Neithwyr worked for this Baliasir in some capacity, but I never could find out from anyone exactly what Baliasir's line of business was, nor what Neithwyr did for him. Zenithar, the God of Work and Commerce, is the most revered deity in Kambria, which served my (that is to say our) purposes well, as the people are naturally receptive to bribery. Still, it did me little good. I could find nothing specific about our quarry. After days of inquiry, an old crone recommended that I go to a nearby village called Grimtry Garden, and find the cemetery caretaker there. I set off at once.

I know you are impatient when it comes to details, and have little taste for Breton architecture, but if you ever find yourself in mid–High Rock, you owe it to yourself to visit this quaint village. Like a number of other similar towns in High Rock, there is a high wall surrounded it. As well as being picturesque, it's a remnant of the region's turbulent past and a useful barrier against the supernatural creatures that sometimes stalk the countryside. More about that in a moment.

The cemetery is actually outside of the city gates, I discovered. The locals warned me to wait until morning to speak to the caretaker, but I was impatient for information, and did not want to waste a moment. I trekked through the woods to the lonely graveyard, and immediately found the shuffling, elderly man who was the caretaker. He bade me leave, that the land was haunted and if I chose to stay I would be in the greatest danger. I told him that I would not go until he told me what he knew about Hadwaf Neithwyr and his patron Baliasir. On hearing their names, he fled deeper into the jumble of broken tombstones and decrepit mausoleums. I naturally pursued.

I saw him scramble down into an enormous crypt and gave chase. There was no light within, but I had planned enough to bring with me a torch. The minute I lit it, I heard a long, savage howl pierce the silence, and I knew that the caretaker had left quickly not merely because he feared speaking of Neithwyr and Baliasir. Before I saw the creature, I heard its heavy breath and the clack of its clawed feet on stone moving closer to me. The werewolf emerged from the gloom, brown and black, with slavering jaws, looking at me with the eyes of the cemetery caretaker, now given only to animal hunger.

I instantly had three different instinctive reactions. The first was, of course, flight. The second was to fight. But if I fled, I might never find the caretaker again, and learn what he knew. If I fought, I might injure or even kill the creature and be even worse off.

So I elected to go with my third option: to hold my ground and keep the creature within its tomb until the night became morning, and the caretaker resumed his humanity.

I've sparred often enough unarmored, but surely never with so much at stake, and never with so savage an opponent. My mind was always on danger not only of injury but the dread disease of lycanthropy. Every rake of its claw I parried, every snap of its foaming jaws I ducked. I sidestepped when it tried to rush me, but closed the distance to keep it from escaping into the night. For hours we fought, I always on the defense, it always trying to free itself, or slay me, or both. I have no doubt that a werewolf has greater energy reserves than a man, but it is a beast and does not know how to save and temper its movements. As the dawn rose, we were both nearly unconscious from fatigue, but I received my reward. The creature became a man once again.

He was quite considerably friendlier than he had been before. In fact, when he realized that I had prevented him from going on his nocturnal rampage through the countryside, he became positively affable.

Here's what I learned: Neithwyr never returned to High Rock. As far as the old man knows, he is still in Morrowind. I visited the gravesite of his sister Peryra, and learned that it was probably through her that Neithwyr first met his patron. It would seem that she was quite a well-known courtesan in her day, and very well traveled, though she chose to return home to die. Unlike Neithwyr, Baliasir is not far away from me. He is a shadowy character, but lately, according to the caretaker, he has been paying court to Queen Elysana in Wayrest. I leave at once.

Please write to me as soon as possible to tell me of your progress. I should be in Wayrest at the home of my friend Lady Elysbetta Moorling in a week's time. If Baliasir is at court, Lady Moorling will be able to arrange an introduction.

I feel confident in saying that we are very close to Azura's Star.

Your Friend, Charwich

Book II

3 Last Seed, 3E 411. Tel Aruhn, Morrowind.

My Good Friend Charwich,

I only just last week received your letter dated 6 Sun's Height, addressed to me in Sadrith Mora. I did not know how to reach you before to tell you of my progress finding Hadwaf Neithwyr, so I send this to you now care of the lady you mentioned in your letter, the Lady Elysbetta Moorling of Wayrest. I hope that if you have left her palace, she will know where you've gone and can send this to you. And I hope further that you receive it in a timelier manner that I received your letter. It is essential that I hear from you soon so we may coordinate our next course of action.

My adventures here have two acts, one before I received your letter, and one immediately after. While you searched for the elusive possessor of Azura's Star in his homeland to the west, I searched for him here where we understood he conjured up the Daedra Prince and received from her the artifact.

Like you, I had little difficulty finding people who had heard of or even knew Neithwyr. In fact, not long after we parted company and you left for the Iliac Bay, I met someone who knew where he went to perform the ceremony, so I left at once to come here to Tel Aruhn. It took some time to locate my contact, for he is a Dissident Priest named Minerath. The Temple and Tribunal, the real powers of Morrowind, tend to frown on his Order, and while they haven't begun so much of crusade to stamp them out, there are certainly rumors that they will soon. This tends to make priests like Minerath skittish and paranoid. Difficult people to set appointments with.

Finally I was told that he would be willing to talk to me at the Plot and Plaster, a tiny tavern without even a room to rent. Downstairs, there were several cloaked men crammed around the tavern's only table, and they searched me to see if I had any weaponry. Of course, I hadn't. You know that isn't my preferred method of doing business.

When it decided that I was harmless, one of the cloaked figures revealed himself to be Minerath. I paid him the gold I promised and asked him what he knew about Hadwaf Neithwyr. He remembered him well enough, saying that after he received the Star, the lad intended to return to High Rock. It seemed he had unfinished business there, presumably of a violent nature, which Azura's Star would facilitate. He had no other information, and I did not know what else to ask.

We parted company and I waited for your letter, hoping you had found Neithwyr and perhaps even the Star. I confess that as I lingered in Morrowind and never heard from you, I began to have doubts about your character. You'll forgive me for saying so, but I began to fear that you had taken the artifact for yourself. In fact, I was making plans to come to High Rock myself when your letter came at last.

The tale of your adventure in the cemetery at Grimtry Garden, and the information you gathered from the lycanthropic caretaker inspired me to have another meeting with Minerath. Thus began the second act of my story.

I returned to the Pot and Plaster, reasoning that the priest must frequent that area of the city to feel so comfortable setting clandestine meetings there. It took some time searching, but I finally found him, and as luck would have it, he was alone. I called his name, and he quickly drew me to a dark alleyway, nervous that we would be seen by a Temple ordinator.

It is a rare and beautiful thing when a victim insists on dragging his killer to a remote location.

I began at once asking about this fellow you mentioned, Neithwyr's mysterious patron Baliasir. He denied ever having heard the name. We were still in that easy, fairly conversational state when I attacked the priest. Of course, he was completely taken by surprise. In some ways, that can be more effective than an ambush from behind. No matter how many times I've done it, no one ever expected the friendly man they're talking to grip them by the neck.

I pressed hard against my favorite spot in the soft part of the throat, just below the thyroid cartilage, and it took him too long to react to my lunge and try pushing back. He began to lose consciousness, and I whispered that if I released my grip a little so he could talk and breath, but he tried to call for help, I would snap his neck. He nodded, and I relaxed the pressure, just a bit.

I asked him again about Baliasir, and he shook his head, insisting that he had never heard the name. As frightened as he was, it seemed most likely that he was telling the truth, so I asked him more generally if he knew anyone else who might know something about Hadwaf Neithwyr. He told me that there was a woman present also during the ceremony, someone he introduced as his sister.

I remembered then the part of your letter about seeing the grave of Neithwyr's sister, Peryra. When I mentioned the name to the priest he nodded frantically, but I could see that the interrogation had reached an ending. There is, after all, something about being throttled that causes a man to answer yes to every question. I snapped Minerath's neck, and returned home.

So now I'm again unsure how to proceed. I've made several more inquiries and several of the same people who met Neithwyr remember him being with a woman. A few recall him saying that she was his sister. One or two believe they remember her name as being Peryra, though they're not certain. No one, however, has heard of anyone named Baliasir.

If I do not hear word from you in response to this in the next couple of weeks, I will come to High Rock, because it's there that most people believe Neithwyr returned. I will only stay here long enough to see if there are other inquiries I can make only in Morrowind to bring us closer to our goal of recovering Azura's Star.

Your Friend,

Koniinge

Book III

13 Last Seed, 3E 411 Wayrest, High Rock

My Dear Koniinge,

Please forgive the quality of the handwriting on this note, but I have not long to live. I can only reply in detail to one part of your letter, and that is that I fear Baliasir, contrary to what you've heard, is very much real. Had he been but a figment of that caretaker's imagination, I would not be feeling life ebb from me as I write this.

Lady Moorling has sent for healers, but I know they won't arrive in time. I just need to explain what happened so that you'll understand, and then all my affairs in this world will be ended. The one advantage of my condition is that I must be brief, without my habitually ornamental descriptions of people and places. I know that you will appreciate that at least.

It started when I came to Wayrest, and through my friend Lady Moorling and her court connections was introduced to Baliasir himself. I had to proceed carefully, not wanting him to know of our designs on Azura's Star which I presumed he possessed, given to him by his servant Hadwaf Neithwyr. His function in Queen Elysana's court seemed to be decorative, like so many of her courtiers, and it was not hard to differentiate myself from the others when we began conversing on the school of mysticism. Many of the other hangers-on at the palace can speak eloquently on the subject of the magickal arts, but it seemed that only he and I had deep knowledge of the craft.

Many a nobleman or adventurer who aren't mages by profession learn a spell or two from the useful schools of restoration or destruction. I told Baliasir quite truthfully that I had never learned any of that (oh, but I wish I knew some healing spells of the school of restoration now), but that I had developed some small skill in mysticism. Not enough to be a Psijic, of course, but in telekinesis, password, and spell reflection I had some amateur ability. He responded with compliments, which allowed me to segue into the topic of another spell of mysticism, the soul trap.

I told him I was unlearned but curious about that spell. And very naturally and comfortably, I was able to bring up the subject of Azura's Star, the endless well of souls.

Imagine how I had to hold back my excitement when he leaned in and whispered to me, "If that interests you, come to Klythic's Cairn west of the city tomorrow night."

I couldn't sleep at all. The only thing I could think of was how I would get the Star when he showed it to me. I still knew so little about Baliasir, his past and his power, but the opportunity was too great to let pass. Still, I must admit that I held hopes that you would arrive, as you threatened you might in your letter, so I might have someone of physical strength to aid me in my adventure.

I am growing weaker and weaker as I write this, so I must proceed with the basic facts. I went to the crypt the following night, and Baliasir led me through the maze of it to the repository where he kept the Star. We were talking quite casually, and as you've so often said, it seemed an excellent time for an ambush. I grabbed the Star and unsheathed my blade in what I felt was amazing speed.

He turned to me and I suddenly felt that I was moving like a snail. In a flash, Baliasir changed his form and became his true self, not man or mer, but daedra. A colossal daedra lord who swiped back the Star from my grasp and laughed at my sword as it thudded against his impenetrable hide.

I knew I had been beaten, and I threw myself towards the corridor. A blue flash of energy coursed through me, flung by Baliasir's claws. At once, I began to feel death. He could have smote me with a thousand spells, but he chose the one where I could lie down, and suffer, and hear him laugh. At the very least, I did not give him that pleasure.

Already struck, it was too late for me to cast a counterspell of mysticism, one to dispel the magicka, reflect it or absorb it as my own. But I did still know how to teleport myself, what mystics term 'Recall,' to whatever place I'd last set a spiritual anchor. I confess that at the time, I didn't remember where that would be. Perhaps in Bhoriane when I arrived in the Iliac Bay, or in Kambria, or in Grimtry Garden where I met the caretaker, or my hostess's palace in Wayrest. I prayed that I had not set the anchor last when I was with you in Morrowind, for it said that if the distance is too great, one can be caught between dimensions. Still, I was willing to take that chance, rather than being the plaything of Baliasir.

I cast the spell and found myself back on the doorstep of Lady Moorling's palace. To be out of the crypt and away from the daedra was a relief, but I had so hoped that I had been smart enough to cast an anchor near a Mages Guild or a temple where I could find a healer. Instead, knowing I was too weak to walk far, I beat on the door and was taken here, where I write this letter, lying in my bed.

As I wrote those words, dear Elysbetta, Lady Moorling, came in, quite tearfully and frantic, to tell me the healers should be hre withn but a few minute. But I wil be ded ere they arrve. I know thes are m last wors. Der frend, stay away frm this cursd place.

Yr Frend,

Charwich

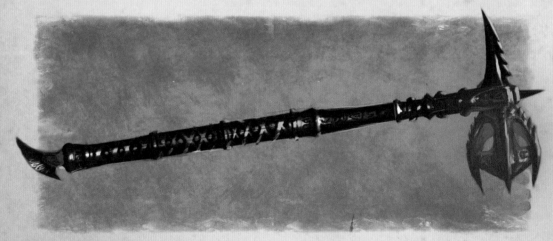

Book IV

8 Sun's Dawn, 3E 412. Amiglith, Summurset Isle.

My Good Friend, Lord Gemyn,

You must forgive me for not meeting you at the palace personally, but I've been unavoidably, tragically detained. I've left the front gate and door unlocked, and if you're reading this, you must have made it at least as far the antechamber to the east drawing room. Perhaps you've already wandered the estate and seen some of its delights before coming to this chamber: the seven fountains of marble and porphyry, the reflecting pool, the various groves, the colonnades and quincunx. I don't think you would have already gone to the second floor suites and the west wing as you would have had to pass this room first, and picked up this letter. But believe me, they're beautifully appointed with magnificent balustrades, winding staircases, intimate salons, and bedchambers worthy of your affluence.

The price of this property is exorbitant, certainly, but for a man like you who seeks only the best, this is the villa you must have. As you undoubtedly noticed as you arrived through the gates, there are several smaller buildings ideally suited to be guard stations. I know you are concerned with security.

I am an intensely greedy man, and there is nothing I would have liked more than to meet you here today, show you the grounds, fawn on you obsequiously, and collect a fat percentage of the cost of the sale when you bought this marvelous palace, as I'm sure you would have. My dilemma that caused my inexcusable absence began shortly after I arrived here early to make certain the villa was well-cleaned for your inspection. A man named Koniinge crept up behind me, and gripped me by the throat. Clamping his left hand over my mouth and nose, and throttling me with his right hand, crushing the soft spot on my throat just below the thyroidal cartilage, he effectively strangled me in a few quick but very painful minutes.

I am currently buried in a pile of leaves in the north statuary parterre, close to the exceptional sculptural representation of the Transformation of Trinimac. It should not be too long before I am discovered: someone at my bank will surely notice my absence in due time. Koniinge might have buried me deeper, but he wanted to be ready for the arrival of his old partner, Charwich.

Perhaps part of you thinks it best to stop reading now, Lord Gemyn. You are looking around the antechamber and seeing nothing but doors. The large one you took to come in from the garden is locked now behind you, and without a better knowledge of the layout of the estate, I could not recommend you attempt to flee down a corridor that might easily come to a dead end. No. Much better to keep reading, and see where this is going.

THE SKYRIM LIBRARY: VOLUME III

Koniinge, it seems, was in a partnership with his friend Charwich to try to recover Azura's Star. They understood it to be in the possession of someone named Hadwaf Neithwyr, a man who conjured up the Daedra Prince Azura herself to acquire it. As Neithwyr originally haled from High Rock, Charwich went there to look for him, while his partner searched Morrowind. They planned to communicate their findings by letters sent through couriers.

Charwich's first letter stated that he had found information that Neithwyr had a mysterious patron named Baliasir, a fact he had learned at a cemetery with a gravestone of Neithwyr's sister Peryra and a lycanthropic caretaker. Koniinge replied back that he could find nothing about Baliasir, but believed that Neithwyr had returned to High Rock with Peryra after getting the Star. Charwich's last letter was a written on his deathbed, having sustained mortal wounds from his battle with Baliasir, who it seemed had been a mighty daedra lord.

Koniinge grieved for his friend, and traveled the span of the Empire to Wayrest, to pay his call of condolences on Lady Moorling, the woman at whose house Charwich had been staying. After making some inquiries, Koniinge learned that her ladyship had left the city, quite suddenly. She had been entertaining a guest named Charwich, and it was understood that he had died, though no one ever saw the body. Certainly no healers had been sent to her house on the 13th of Last Seed of last year. And no one in Wayrest, just like no one in Tel Aruhn, had ever heard of Baliasir.

Poor Koniinge was suddenly unsure of everything. He retraced his late partner's path through Boriane and Grimtry Gardens, but found that the Neithwyr family crypt was elsewhere, in a small town in the barony of Dwynnen. There was indeed a lycanthropic caretaker, fortunately in human form at the time. When questioned (using the technique of strangulation, release, strangulation, release), he told Koniinge the story that he had told Charwich many months before.

Hadwaf and Peryra Neithwyr had returned to Dwynnen, intent on settling old business. As the Star requires potent spirits for power, they thought they would begin small by capturing the spirit of the werewolf they knew of in the family graveyard. Sadly, for them, their grasp exceeded their reach. When the poor caretaker resumed his human form one morning, he found himself lying next to the shredded, bloody bodies of the Neithwyr siblings. Distressed and fearful, he brought the corpses and all their possessions down into the crypt. They were still there when Charwich came, and so too was Azura's Star.

Koniinge now saw things clearly. The letters he had received from Charwich were lies, intended to keep him away. Undoubtedly with the assistance of Lady Moorling, his new partner, he had concocted stories, including one of his own demise, to trick Koniinge into abandoning the quest for the Star. It was clearly a sad statement on the nature of friendship, and one that needed immediate correction.

It took the better part of six months for Koniinge to find his old partner. Charwich and Lady Moorling had used the power of the Star to make themselves very wealthy and powerful. They assumed a number of different identities in their travels through High Rock and Skyrim, and then down to Valenwood and the Summurset Isle. Along the way, of course, the Star itself disappeared, as great daedric artifacts always do. The couple still had much wealth, but their love sadly fell on troubled times. When they reached Alinor, they parted ways.

One must assume that during their months together, Charwich must have told Lady Moorling about Koniinge. It's pleasant to think of the loving couple laughing over the stories they were telling him about the mythical and dangerous Baliasir. Charwich must not have given his former beloved a very accurate physical description, however, because when Lady Moorling (then under the identity of the Countess Zyliana) met Koniinge, she had no idea who he was. It came as quite a surprise to her when he began strangling her and requesting information about her former paramour.

Before she died, she told Koniinge what Charwich's new name and title was, and where he was looking for a new palace. She even told him about me. Given all the twists and bends the last months' chase took him on, it was not difficult to find which palace Charwich was looking to buy, and what time his appointment was to view it. Then he had merely to arrive early, dispose of me, and wait.

There our story must sadly end. I look forward to seeing you soon.
Yours,

Syrix Goinithi, Former Estate Banker

P.S.: Charwich — Turn around now, or don't. Your choice. Your friend, Koniinge.

On the Great Collapse

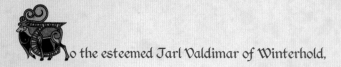o the esteemed Jarl Valdimar of Winterhold,

First, please allow me to offer my most sincere condolences. I understand that you, like many others, have lost family and you have my deepest sympathies.

I also understand that some on your council have placed the blame for this horrible disaster on my colleagues at the College. While I can certainly appreciate the shock at the scope of recent events, and the desire to comprehend what has happened, I must strongly urge you to consider the full situation.

You know as well as any the College's history and reputation in Winterhold. It has long been a source of pride for your city, a unique fixture in Skyrim. Some of the greatest wizards have studied here, and the College has always promoted positive relations with the other provinces of Tamriel.

It is well-known that those relations have been, shall we say, strained over the last few decades. After the Oblivion Crisis, it was only natural that the people of Skyrim showed a distrust for mages, even though the vast majority of us actively worked to counter the actions of the Mythic Dawn cult. The College expected such a reaction, and hoped that distrust would fade over time.

And then, the Red Year. No one foresaw the explosion of Red Mountain, or the devastating effect it would have on the Dunmer culture. Your predecessor was kind enough to welcome many of the refugees, particularly those who could contribute to the College's studies. We were quite grateful.

When Solstheim was generously offered to the Dunmer as a new home, I was as surprised as any. I did not, however, share the apparent expectation that all dark elves would leave Skyrim. It did not go unnoticed that many in Winterhold were unhappy at how many mages chose to stay at the College rather than relocate.

And now, the storms that have wracked the coast of Skyrim for close to a year have finally broken, but at great cost to us all. This great collapse that has devastated Winterhold was unexpected, I assure you. That the College has remained unaffected is only a testament to the protective magicks placed around it so long ago. It in no way implies that we were somehow prepared specifically for this event, and is certainly no indication that the College was somehow responsible.

I certainly would never hold you accountable for the gossip spread amongst the people of Winterhold. I would urge you, though, to not allow that gossip to take root and become a commonly held belief. I do not wish to see our relationship crumble like Winterhold has, as I assure you the College will remain here a very, very long time.

Your persistent advocate,

Arch-Mage Deneth

The Apprentice's Assistant

Advice from Valenwood's most prestigious spellcaster

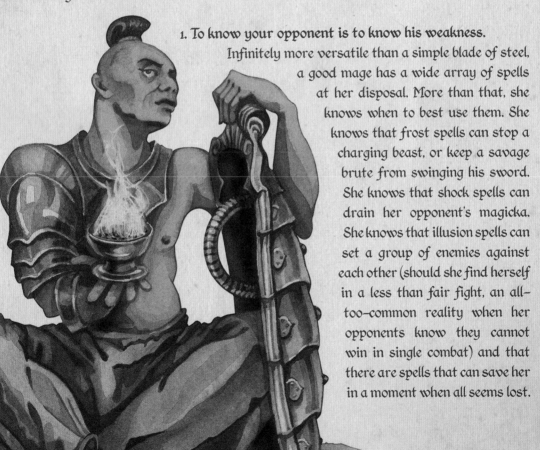

No doubt you have heard tales of my adventures. Stories carried from province to province, all of Tamriel in awe of my feats of magical prowess. More than once, I am sure, you have thought "if only I had Aramril's ability. Then I too could seek fame and fortune in magic duels!"

It is true, of course. Great fame and limitless fortune await those who are successful. But to be successful, one needs to learn from the best. That is why you have purchased this book, so that I may teach you. I am, of course, the best.

Here, then, is my advice. Follow it, and you too can make a name for yourself throughout Tamriel.

1. To know your opponent is to know his weakness.

Infinitely more versatile than a simple blade of steel, a good mage has a wide array of spells at her disposal. More than that, she knows when to best use them. She knows that frost spells can stop a charging beast, or keep a savage brute from swinging his sword. She knows that shock spells can drain her opponent's magicka. She knows that illusion spells can set a group of enemies against each other (should she find herself in a less than fair fight, an all-too-common reality when her opponents know they cannot win in single combat) and that there are spells that can save her in a moment when all seems lost.

2. To know yourself is to know your limits.

Even the best mage has a finite reserve of magicka; none born yet have been graced with Magnus' infinite reserves of power. And so a good mage does not over-extend herself. She makes sure she always has enough magicka to keep herself safe. Failing that, she makes sure she has a sizable supply of potions at the ready. Failing that, she makes sure she always has an escape route. Not that the Great Aramril has ever fled a fight, but of course you do not necessarily share her superb natural ability. That is why you must practice.

3. Wards can kill (you)

There is no question that wards are an essential tool of any aspiring mage. They can block incoming spells, negating your opponent's attack and wasting his magicka. A good mage knows, however, to not rely too heavily on her ward. Keeping a ward readied for too long will leave a caster drained of magicka, unable to retaliate, and at worst unable to maintain the ward and therefore completely defenseless.

4. Two hands are not always better than one

Any advanced spellcaster has learned to cast spells with both hands, dealing more damage. There are certainly times when this is to your advantage, such as when an opponent is already weakened, or when it is likely to draw a bigger reaction from the crowd that has no doubt gathered to watch you. It is not always the best strategy, however. Concentration spells, for example, can often be used on the ground when an opponent is especially nimble. In that instance, using both hands independently can cover more ground at the same time. A mage throwing fireballs with both hands cannot immediately raise a ward to defend herself, or heal while she continues to attack.

5. Always rise to a challenge, especially when you know you can win

Remember that your first priority is, of course, to stay alive. Following closely behind, though, is your need to please the crowd. You are, after all, depending on their generosity to fund your adventures. Here, then, more than magic comes into play. If you can gain a sense of your opponent's ability before the duel begins, you can enter into the event with confidence. Knowing that you outclass your opponent is of great importance, as it means you can confidently give the crowd a better show. Likewise, knowing ahead of time that you could very well lose a duel, you are afforded an opportunity to suddenly find yourself engaged elsewhere, and be unable to attend the event. (By no means do I suggest that I have ever done such a thing; I simply find that my great fame occasionally means I am unable to respond to every single request for a duel)

Keep these few things in mind, keep your wits about you, and you too can make a name for yourself by putting on great displays of magical prowess. Take care, though — for if you become successful enough, you may find yourself facing a challenge from me!

The Final Lesson

By Aegrothius Goth

"It is time for you to leave your apprenticeship here," said the Great Sage to his students, Taksim and Vonguldak.

"So soon?" cried Vonguldak, for it had been but a few years since the training began, "Are we such poor pupils?"

"We have learned much for you, master, but you have no more to teach us?" Taksim asked. "You have told us so many tales of great enchanters of the past. Can't we continue to learn until we have reached some level of their power?"

"I have one last story for you," smiled the Great Sage.

Many thousands of years ago, long before the Cyrodilic Dynasty of Reman and even longer before the Septim Dynasty ruled Tamriel, and before there was a Mages Guild, and when the land called Morrowind was known as Resdayn, and the land of Elsweyr was called Anequina and Pellitine, and the only law of the land was the cruel ways of the Alessian Doctrines of Marukh, there lived a hermetic enchanter named Dalak who had two apprentices, Uthrac and Loreth.

Uthrac and Loreth were remarkable students, both equally assiduous in their learning, the pride of their Master. Both excelled at the arts of the cauldron, mirror castings, the infusion of spiritas into mundus, and the weaving of air and fire. Dalak was very fond of his boys, and they of him.

On a springtide morn, Dalak received a message from another enchanter named Peothil, who lived deep in the forests of the Colovian heartland. You must remember that in the dark days of the First Era, mages were solitary practitioners with the only organized consortium being the Psijics of Artaeum. Away from that island, mages seldom saw one another and even more rarely corresponded. Thus, when Dalak received Peothil's letter, he gave it his great attention.

Peothil was greatly aged, and he had found the peace of his isolation threatened by the Alessian Reform. He feared for his life, knowing that the fanatical priests and their warriors were close at hand. Dalak brought his students to him.

"It will be an arduous and perilous journey to the Colovian Estates, one that I would fear partaking even in my youth," Dalak said. "My heart trembles to send you two forth to Peothil's cave, but I know that he is a great and benevolent enchanter, and his light must continue to burn in the heart of the continent if we are to survive these dark nights."

Uthrac and Loreth pled with their teacher not to order them to go to Peothil. It was not the priests and warriors of the Alessian Reform they feared, but they knew their Master was aged and infirm, and could not protect himself if the Reform moved further westward. Finally, he relented and allowed that one would stay with him, and the other would journey forth to the Colovian Estates. He would let them decide which of them would go.

The lads debated and discussed, fought and compromised, and at last elected to let fate make the choice. They threw lots, and Loreth came up short. He left early the next morning, miserable and filled with fear.

For a month and a day, he tramped through the forests into the midst of the Colovian Estates. Through some planning, some skill, and much assistance for sympathetic peasants, he managed to avoid the ever-tightening circle of the Alessian Reform by crossing through unclaimed mountain passes and hidden bogs. When at last he found the dark caverns where Dalak had told him to search for Peothil, it was still many hours before he could find the enchanter's lair.

No one appeared to be there. Loreth searched through the laboratory of ancient tomes, cauldrons and crystalline flutes, herbs kept alive by the glow of mystic circles, strange liquids and gasses caught in transparent membranes. At last, he found Peothil, or so he presumed. The desiccated shell on the floor of the study, clutching

tools of enchantment, scarcely seemed human.

Loreth decided that he could do nothing further for the mage, and began at once the journey back to his true master Dalak and his friend Uthrac. The armies of the Reform had moved quickly since he passed. After more than one close near encounter, the young enchanter realized that he was trapped on all sides. The only retreat that was possible was back in the caves of Peothil.

The first thing to be done, Loreth saw, was to find a means to keep the army from finding the laboratory. That, he found, was what Peothil himself had been trying to do, but by a simple error even an apprentice enchanter could recognize, he had only succeeded in destroying himself. Loreth was able to take what he had learned from Dalak and apply it to Peothil's enchantments, quite successfully. The laboratory was never found or even detected by the Reform.

Much time passed. In the 480th year of the First Era, the great Aiden Direnni won many battles against the Alessian horde, and many passages and routes that had once been closed were now open. Loreth, now no longer young, was able to return to Dalak.

When at last he found his way to his Master's old hovel, he saw candles of mourning lit in all the trees surrounding. Even before he knocked on the door and met his old fellow student Uthrac, Loreth knew that Dalak had died.

"It was only a few months ago," said Uthrac, after embracing his friend. "He talked of you every day of every year you were away. Somehow he knew that you had not preceded him to the world beyond. He told me that you would come back."

The gray-haired men sat before the fire and reminisced of the old days. The sad truth was that they both discovered how different they had become. Uthrac spoke of carrying on the Master's work, while Loreth described his new discoveries. They left one another that day, each shaking his head, destined to never see one another again.

In the years ahead, before they left the mortal world to join their great teacher Dalak, they both achieved their desires. Uthrac went on to become respected if minor enchanter in the service of Clan Direnni. Loreth took the skills he had learned on his own, and used them to fashion the Balac-thurm, the Staff of Chaos.

My boys, the lesson is you have to learn from a teacher to avoid those small but essential errors that claimed the life of such self-taught enchanters as Peothil. And yet, the only way to become truly great is to try all the possibilities on your own.

Feyfolken

by Waughin Jarth

Book One

The Great Sage was a tall, untidy man, bearded but bald. His library resembled him: all the books had been moved over the years to the bottom shelves where they gathered in dusty conglomerations. He used several of the books in his current lecture, explaining to his students, Taksim and Vonguldak, how the Mages Guild had first been founded by Vanus Galerion. They had many questions about Galerion's beginnings in the Psijic Order, and how the study of magic there differed from the Mages Guild.

"It was, and is, a very structured way of life," explained the Great Sage. "Quite elitist, actually. That was the aspect of it Galerion most objected to. He wanted the study of magic to be free. Well, not free exactly, but at least available to all who could afford it. In doing that, he changed the course of life in Tamriel."

"He codified the praxes and rituals used by all modern potionmakers, itemmakers, and spellmakers, didn't he, Great Sage?" asked Vonguldak.

"That was only part of it. Magic as we know it today comes from Vanus Galerion. He restructured the schools to be understandable by the masses. He invented the tools of alchemy and enchanting so everyone could concoct whatever they wanted, whatever their skills and purse would allow them to, without fears of magical backfire. Well, eventually he created that."

"What do you mean, Great Sage?" asked Taksim.

"The first tools were more automated than the ones we have today. Any layman could use them without the least understanding of enchantment and alchemy. On the Isle of Artaeum, the students had to learn the skills laboriously and over many years, but Galerion decided that was another example of the Psijics' elitism. The tools he invented were like robotic master enchanters and alchemists, capable of creating anything the customer required, provided he could pay."

"So someone could, for example, create a sword that would cleave the world in twain?" asked Vonguldak.

"I suppose, in theory, but it would probably take all the gold in the world," chuckled the Great Sage. "No, I can't say we were ever in very great danger, but that it isn't to say that there weren't a few unfortunate incidents where a unschooled yokel invented something beyond his ken. Eventually, of course, Galerion tore apart his old tools, and created what we use today. It's a little elitist, requiring that people know what they're doing before they do it, but remarkably practical."

"What did people invent?" asked Taksim. "Are there any stories?"

"You're trying to distract me so I don't test you," said the Great Sage. "But I suppose I can tell you one story, just to illustrate a point. This particular tale takes place in city of Alinor on the west coast of Summurset Isle, and concerns a scribe named Thaurbad.

This was in the Second Era, not long after Vanus Galerion had first founded the Mages Guild and chapter houses had sprung up all over Summurset, though not yet spread to the mainland of Tamriel.

For five years, this scribe, Thaurbad, had conducted all his correspondence to the outside world by way of his messenger boy, Gorgos. For the first year of his adoption of the hermit life, his few remaining friends and family — friends and family of his dead wife, truth be told — had tried visiting, but even the most indefatigable kin gives up eventually when given no encouragement. No one had a good reason to keep in touch with Thaurbad Hulzik, and in time, very few even tried. His sister-in-law sent him the occasional letter with news of people he could barely remember, but even that communication was rare. Most of messages to and from his house dealt with his business, writing the weekly proclamation from the Temple of Auri-El. These were bulletins nailed on the temple door, community news, sermons, that sort of thing.

The first message Gorgos brought him that day was from his healer, reminding him of his appointment on Turdas. Thaurbad took a while to write his response, glum and affirmative. He had the Crimson Plague, which he was being treated for at considerable expense — you have to remember these were the days before the School of Restoration had become quite so specialized. It was a dreadful disease and had taken away his voicebox. That was why he only communicated by script.

The next message was from Alfiers, the secretary at the church, as curt and noxious as ever: "THAURBAD, ATTACHED IS SUNDAS'S SERMON, NEXT WEEK'S EVENTS CALENDAR, AND THE OBITUARIES. TRY TO LIVEN THEM UP A LITTLE. I WASN'T HAPPY WITH YOUR LAST ATTEMPT."

Thaurbad had taken the job putting together the Bulletin before Alfiers joined the temple, so his only mental image of her was purely theoretical and had evolved over time. At first he thought of Alfiers as an ugly fat sloadess covered with warts; more recently, she had mutated into a rail-thin, spinster orcess. Of course, it was possible his clairvoyance was accurate and she had just lost weight.

Whatever Alfiers looked like, her attitude towards Thaurbad was clear, unwavering disdain. She hated his sense of humor, always found the most minor of misspellings, and considered his structure and calligraphy the worst kind of amateur work. Luckily, working for a temple was the next most secure job to working for the good King of Alinor. It didn't bring in very much money, but his expenses were minimal. The truth was, he didn't need to do it anymore. He had quite a fortune stashed away, but he didn't have anything else to occupy his days. And the truth was further that having little else to occupy his time and thoughts, the Bulletin was very important to him.

Gorgos, having delivered all the messages, began to clean and as he did so, he told

Thaurbad all the news in town. The boy always did so, and Thaurbad seldom paid him any attention, but this time he had an interesting report. The Mages Guild had come to Alinor.

As Thaurbad listened intently, Gorgos told him all about the Guild, the remarkable Archmagister, and the incredible tools of alchemy and enchanting. Finally, when the lad had finished, Thaurbad scribbled a quick note and handed it and a quill to Gorgos. The note read, "Have them enchant this quill."

"It will be expensive," said Gorgos.

Thaurbad gave Gorgos a sizeable chunk of the thousands of gold pieces he had saved over the years, and sent him out the door. Now, Thaurbad decided, he would finally have the ability to impress Alfiers and bring glory to the Temple of Auri-El.

The way I've heard the story, Gorgos had thought about taking the gold and leaving Alinor, but he had come to care for poor old Thaurbad. And even more, he hated Alfiers who he had to see every day to get his messages for his master. It wasn't perhaps for the best of motivations, but Gorgos decided to go to the Guild and get the quill enchanted.

The Mages Guild was not then, especially not then, an elitist institution, as I have said, but when the messenger boy came in and asked to use the Itemmaker, he was greeted with some suspicion. When he showed the bag of gold, the attitude melted, and he was ushered in the room.

Now, I haven't seen one of the enchanting tools of old, so you must use your imagination. There was a large prism for the item to be bound with magicka, assuredly, and an assortment of soul gems and globes of trapped energies. Other than that, I cannot be certain how it looked or how it worked. Because of all the gold he gave to the Guild, Gorgos could infuse the quill with the highest-price soul available, which was something daedric called Feyfolken. The initiate at the Guild, being ignorant as most Guildmembers were at that time, did not know very much about the spirit except that it was filled with energy. When Gorgos left the room, the quill had been enchanted to its very limit and then some. It was virtually quivering with power.

Of course, when Thaurbad used it, that's when it became clear how over his head he was.

And now," said the Great Sage. "It's time for your test."

"But what happened? What were the quill's powers?" cried Taksim.

"You can't stop the tale there!" objected Vonguldak.

"We will continue the tale after your conjuration test, provided you both perform exceptionally well," said the Great Sage.

Book Two

After the test had been given and Vonguldak and Taksim had demonstrated their knowledge of elementary conjuration, the Great Sage told them that they were free to enjoy the day. The two lads, who most afternoons fidgeted through their lessons, refused to leave their seats.

"You told us that after the test, you'd tell us more of your tale about the scribe and his enchanted quill," said Taksim.

"You've already told us about the scribe, how he lived alone, and his battles with the Temple secretary over the Bulletin he scripted for posting, and how he suffered from the Crimson Plague and couldn't speak. When you left off, his messenger boy had just had his master's quill enchanted with the spirit of a daedra named Feyfolken," added Vonguldak to aid the Great Sage's memory.

"As it happens," said the Great Sage. "I was thinking about a nap. However, the story does touch on some issues of the natures of spirits and thus is related to conjuration, so I'll continue.

Thaurbad began using the quill to write the Temple Bulletin, and there was something about the slightly lopsided, almost three-dimensional quality of the letters that Thaurbad liked a lot.

Into the night, Thaurbad put together the Temple of Auri-El's Bulletin. For the moment he washed over the page with the Feyfolken quill, it became a work of art, an illuminated manuscript crafted of gold, but with good, simple and strong vernacular. The sermon excerpts read like poetry, despite being based on the archpriest's workmanlike exhortation of the most banal of the Alessian doctrines. The obituaries of two of the Temple's chief benefactors were stark and powerful, pitifully mundane deaths transitioned into world-class tragedies. Thaurbad worked the magical palette until he nearly fainted from exhaustion. At six o'clock in the morning, a day before deadline, he handed the Bulletin to Gorgos for him to carry to Alfiers, the Temple secretary.

As expected, Alfiers never wrote back to compliment him or even comment on how early he had sent the bulletin. It didn't matter. Thaurbad knew it was the best Bulletin the Temple had ever posted. At one o'clock on Sundas, Gorgos brought him many messages.

"The Bulletin today was so beautiful, when I read it in the vestibule, I'm ashamed to tell you I wept copiously," wrote the archpriest. "I don't think I've seen anything that captures Auri-El's glory so beautifully before. The cathedrals of Firsthold pale in comparison. My friend, I prostrate myself before the greatest artist since Gallael."

The archpriest was, like most men of the cloth, given to hyperbole. Still, Thaurbad was happy with the compliment. More messages followed. All of the Temple Elders and thirty-three of the parishioners young and old had all taken the time to find out who wrote the bulletin and how to get a message to congratulate him. And there was only one person they could go through for that information: Alfiers. Imaging the dragon lady besieged by his admirers filled Thaurbad with positive glee.

He was still in a good mood the next day when he took the ferry to his appointment with his healer, Telemichiel. The herbalist was new, a pretty Redguard woman who tried to talk to him, even after he gave her the note reading "My name is Thaurbad Hulzik and I have an appointment with Telemichiel for eleven o'clock. Please forgive me for not talking, but I have no voicebox anymore."

"Has it started raining yet?" she asked cheerfully. "The diviner said it might."

Thaurbad frowned and shook his head angrily. Why was it that everyone thought that mute people liked to be talked to? Did soldiers who lost their arms like to be thrown balls? It was undoubtedly not a purposefully cruel behavior, but Thaurbad still suspected that some people just liked to prove that they weren't crippled too.

The examination itself was routine horror. Telemichiel performed the regular invasive torture, all the while chatting and chatting and chatting.

"You ought to try talking once in a while. That's the only way to see if you're getting better. If you don't feel comfortable doing it in public, you could try practicing it by yourself," said Telemichiel, knowing her patient would ignore her advice. "Try singing in the bath. You'll probably find you don't sound as bad as you think."

Thaurbad left the examination with the promise of test results in a couple of weeks. On the ferry ride back home, Thaurbad began thinking of next week's temple bulletin. What about a double-border around the "Last Sundas's Offering Plate" announcement? Putting the sermon in two columns instead of one might have interesting effects. It was almost unbearable to think that he couldn't get started on it until Alfiers sent him information.

When she did, it was with the note, "LAST BULLETIN A LITTLE BETTER. NEXT TIME, DON'T USE THE WORD 'FORTUITOUS' IN PLACE OF 'FORTUNATE.' THE WORDS ARE NOT, IF YOU LOOK THEM UP, SYNONYMOUS."

In response, Thaurbad almost followed Telemichiel's advice by screaming obscenities at Gorgos. Instead, he drank a bottle of cheap wine, composed and sent a suitable reply, and fell asleep on the floor.

The next morning, after a long bath, Thaurbad began work on the Bulletin. His idea for putting a light shading effect on the "Special Announcements" section had an amazing textural effect. Alfiers always hated the extra decorations he added to the borders, but using the Feyfolken quill, they looked strangely powerful and majestic.

Gorgos came to him with a message from Alfiers at that very moment as if in response to the thought. Thaurbad opened it up. It simply said, "I'M SORRY."

Thaurbad kept working. Alfiers's note he put from his mind, sure that she would soon follow it up with the complete message "I'M SORRY THAT NO ONE EVER TAUGHT YOU TO KEEP RIGHT-HAND AND LEFT-HAND MARGINS THE SAME LENGTH" or "I'M SORRY WE CAN'T GET SOMEONE OTHER THAN A WEIRD, OLD MAN AS SCRIBE OF OUR BULLETIN." It didn't matter what she was sorry about. The columns from the sermon notes rose like the massive pillars of roses, crowned with unashamedly ornate headers. The obituaries and birth announcements were framed together with a spherical border, as a heartbreaking declaration of the circle of life. The Bulletin was simultaneously both warm and avant-garde. It was a masterpiece. When he sent it off to Alfiers late that afternoon, he knew she'd hate it, and was glad.

Thaurbad was surprised to get a message from the Temple on Loredas. Before he read the content, he could tell from the style that it wasn't from Alfiers. The handwriting wasn't Alfiers's usual belligerent slashing style, and it wasn't all in Alfiers's usual capital letters, which read like a scream from Oblivion.

"Thaurbad, I thought you should know Alfiers isn't at the Temple anymore. She quit her position yesterday, very suddenly. My name is Vanderthil, and I was lucky enough (let me admit it now, I begged pitifully) to be your new Temple contact. I'm overwhelmed by your genius. I was having a crisis of faith until I read last week's Bulletin. This week's Bulletin is a miracle. Enough. I just wanted to say I'm honored to be working with you. -- Vanderthil."

The response on Sundas after the service even astonished Thaurbad. The archpriest attributed the massive increase in attendance and collection plate offerings entirely to the Bulletin. Thaurbad's salary was quadrupled. Gorgos brought over a hundred and twenty messages from his adoring public.

The following week, Thaurbad sat in front of his writing plank, a glass of fine Torvali mead at his side, staring at the blank scroll. He had no ideas. The Bulletin, his child, his second-wife, bored him. The third-rate sermons of the archbishop were absolute anathema, and the deaths and births of the Temple patrons struck him as entirely pointless. Blah blah, he thought as he scribbled on the page.

He knew he wrote the letters B-L-A-H B-L-A-H. The words that appeared on the scroll were, "A necklace of pearl on a white neck."

He scrawled a jagged line across the page. It appeared in through that damned beautiful Feyfolken quill: "Glory to Auri-El."

Thaurbad slammed the quill and poetry spilled forth in a stream of ink. He scratched over the page, blotting over everything, and the vanquished words sprung back up in different form, even more exquisite than before. Every daub and splatter caused the document to whirl like a kaleidoscope before falling together in gorgeous asymmetry. There was nothing he could do to ruin the Bulletin. Feyfolken had taken over. He was a reader, not an author.

Now," asked the Great Sage. "What was Feyfolken from your knowledge of the School of Conjuration?"

"What happened next?" cried Vonguldak.

"First, tell me what Feyfolken was, and then I'll continue the story."

"You said it was a daedra," said Taksim. "And it seems to have something to do with artistic expression. Was Feyfolken a servitor of Azura?"

"But the scribe may have been imagining all this," said Vonguldak. "Perhaps Feyfolken is a servitor of Sheogorath, and he's gone mad. Or the quill's writing makes everyone who views it, like all the congregation at the Temple of Auri-El, go mad."

"Hermaeus Mora is the daedra of knowledge ... and Hircine is the daedra of the wild ... and the daedra of revenge is Boethiah," pondered Taksim. And then he smiled, "Feyfolken is a servitor of Clavicus Vile, isn't it?"

"Very good," said the Great Sage. "How did you know?"

"It's his style," said Taksim. "Assuming that he doesn't want the power of the quill now that he has it. What happens next?"

"I'll tell you," said the Great Sage, and continued the tale.

Book Three

Thaurbad had at last seen the power of the quill," said the Great Sage, continuing his tale. "Enchanted with the daedra Feyfolken, servitor of Clavicus Vile, it had brought him great wealth and fame as the scribe of the weekly Bulletin of the Temple of Auri–El. But he realized that it was the artist, and he merely the witness to its magic. He was furious and jealous. With a cry, he snapped the quill in half.

He turned to finish his glass of mead. When he turned around, the quill was intact.

He had no other quills but the one he had enchanted, so he dipped his finger in the inkwell and wrote a note to Gorgos in big sloppy letters. When Gorgos returned with a new batch of congratulatory messages from the Temple, praising his latest Bulletin, he handed the note and the quill to the messenger boy. The note read: "Take the quill back to the Mages Guild and sell it. Buy me another quill with no enchantments."

Gorgos didn't know what to make of the note, but he did as he was told. He returned a few hours later.

"They wouldn't give us any gold back for it," said Gorgos. "They said it wasn't enchanted. I told 'em, I said 'What are you talking about, you enchanted it right here with that Feyfolken soul gem,' and they said, 'Well, there ain't a soul in it now. Maybe you did something and it got loose.'"

Gorgos paused to look at his master. Thaurbad couldn't speak, of course, but he seemed even more than usually speechless.

"Anyway, I threw the quill away and got you this new one, like you said."

Thaurbad studied the new quill. It was white–feathered while his old quill had been dove gray. It felt good in his hand. He sighed with relief and waved his messenger lad away. He had a Bulletin to write, and this time, without any magic except for his own talent.

Within two days time, he was nearly back on schedule. It looked plain but it was entirely his. Thaurbad felt a strange reassurance when he ran his eyes over the page and noticed some slight errors. It had been a long time since the Bulletin contained any errors. In fact, Thaurbad reflected happily, there were probably other mistakes still in the document that he was not seeing.

He was finishing a final whirl of plain calligraphy on the borders when Gorgos arrived with some messages from the Temple. He looked through them all quickly, until one caught his eye. The wax seal on the letter read "Feyfolken." With complete bafflement, he broke it open.

"I think you should kill yourself," it read in perfectly gorgeous script.

He dropped the letter to the floor, seeing sudden movement on the Bulletin. Feyfolken script leapt from the letter and coursed over the scroll in a flood, translating his shabby document into a work of sublime beauty. Thaurbad no longer cared about the weird croaking quality of his voice. He screamed for a very long time. And then drank. Heavily.

Gorgos brought Thaurbad a message from Vanderthil, the secretary of the Temple, early Fredas morning, but it took the scribe until mid-morning to work up the courage to look at it. "Good Morning, I am just checking in on the Bulletin. You usually have it in on Turdas night. I'm curious. You planning something special? — Vanderthil."

Thaurbad responded, "Vanderthil, I'm sorry. I've been sick. There won't be a Bulletin this Sunday" and handed the note to Gorgos before retiring to his bath. When he came back an hour later, Gorgos was just returning from the Temple, smiling.

"Vanderthil and the archpriest went crazy," he said. "They said it was your best work ever."

Thaurbad looked at Gorgos, uncomprehending. Then he noticed that the Bulletin was gone. Shaking, he dipped his finger in the inkwell and scrawled the words "What did the note I sent with you say?"

"You don't remember?" asked Gorgos, holding back a smile. He knew the master had been drinking a lot lately. "I don't remember the exact words, but it was something like, 'Vanderthil, here it is. Sorry it's late. I've been having severe mental problems lately. — Thaurbad.' Since you said, 'here it is,' I figured you wanted me to bring the Bulletin along, so I did. And like I said, they loved it. I bet you get three times as much letters this Sundas."

Thaurbad nodded his head, smiled, and waved the messenger lad away. Gorgos returned back to the Temple, while his master turned to his writing plank, and pulled out a fresh sheet of parchment.

He wrote with the quill: "What do you want, Feyfolken?"

The words became: "Goodbye. I hate my life. I have cut my wrists."

Thaurbad tried another tact: "Have I gone insane?"

The words became: "Goodbye. I have poison. I hate my life."

"Why are you doing this to me?"

"I Thaurbad Hulzik cannot live with myself and my ingratitude. That's why I've put this noose around my neck."

Thaurbad picked up a fresh parchment, dipped his finger in the inkwell, and proceeded to rewrite the entire Bulletin. While his original draft, before Feyfolken had altered it, had been simple and flawed, the new copy was a scrawl. Lower-case I's were undotted, G's looked like Y's, sentences ran into margins and curled up and all over like serpents. Ink from the first page leaked onto the second page. When he yanked the pages from the notebook, a long tear nearly divided the third page in half. Something about the final result was evocative. Thaurbad at least hoped so. He wrote another note reading, simply, "Use this Bulletin instead of the piece of trash I sent you."

When Gorgos returned with new messages, Thaurbad handed the envelope to him. The new letters were all the same, except for one from his healer, Telemichiel. "Thaurbad, we need you to come in as soon as possible. We've received the reports from Black Marsh about a strain of the Crimson Plague that sounds very much like your disease, and we need to re-examine you. Nothing is definite yet, but we're going to want to see what our options are."

It took Thaurbad the rest of the day and fifteen drams of the stoutest mead to recover. The larger part of the next morning was spent recovering from this means of recovery. He started to write a message to Vanderthil: "What did you think of the new Bulletin?" with the quill. Feyfolken's improved version was "I'm going to ignite myself on fire, because I'm a dying no-talent."

Thaurbad rewrote the note using his finger-and-ink message. When Gorgos appeared, he handed him the note. There was one message in Vanderthil's handwriting.

It read, "Thaurbad, not only are you divinely inspired, but you have a great sense of humor. Imagine us using those scribbles you sent instead of the real Bulletin. You made the archbishop laugh heartily. I cannot wait to see what you have next week. Yours fondly, Vanderthil."

The funeral service a week later brought out far more friends and admirers than Thaurbad Hulzik would've believed possible. The coffin, of course, had to be closed, but that didn't stop the mourners from filing into lines to touch its smooth oak surface, imagining it as the flesh of the artist himself. The archbishop managed to rise to the occasion and deliver a better than usual eulogy. Thaurbad's old nemesis, the secretary before Vanderthil, Alfiers came in from Cloudrest, wailing and telling all who would listen that Thaurbad's suggestions had changed the direction of her life. When she heard Thaurbad had left her his quill in his final testament, she broke down in tears. Vanderthil was even more inconsolable, until she found a handsome and delightfully single young man.

"I can hardly believe he's gone and I never even saw him face-to-face or spoke to him," she said. "I saw the body, but even if he hadn't been all burned up, I wouldn't have been able to tell if it was him or not."

"I wish I could tell you there'd been a mistake, but there was plenty of medical evidence," said Telemichiel. "I supplied some of it myself. He was a patient of mine, you see."

"Oh," said Vanderthil. "Was he sick or something?"

"He had the Crimson Plague years ago, that's what took away his voice box, but it appeared to have gone into complete remission. Actually, I had just sent him a note telling him words to that effect the day before he killed himself."

"You're that healer?" exclaimed Vanderthil. "Thaurbad's messenger boy Gorgos told me that he had just picked up that message when I sent mine, complementing him on the new, primative design for the Bulletin. It was amazing work. I never would've told him this, but I had begun to suspect he was stuck in an outmoded style. It turned out he had one last work of genius, before going out in a blaze of glory. Figuratively. And literally."

Vanderthil showed the healer Thaurbad's last Bulletin, and Telemichiel agreed that its frantic, nearly illegible style spoke volumes about the power and majesty of the god Auri-El."

"Now I'm thoroughly confused," said Vonguldak.

"About which part?" asked the Great Sage. "I think the tale is very straight-forward."

"Feyfolken made all the Bulletins beautiful, except for the last one, the one Thaubad did for himself," said Taksim thoughtfully. "But why did he misread the notes from Vanderthil and the healer? Did Feyfolken change those words?"

"Perhaps," smiled the Great Sage.

"Or did Feyfolken changed Thaurbad's perceptions of those words?" asked Vonguldak. "Did Feyfolken make him mad after all?"

"Very likely," said the Great Sage.

"But that would mean that Feyfolken was a servitor of Sheogorath," said Vonguldak. "And you said he was a servitor of Clavicus Vile. Which was he, an agent of mischief or an agent of insanity?"

"The will was surely altered by Feyfolken," said Taksim, "And that's the sort of thing a servitor of Clavicus Vile would do to perpetuate the curse."

"As an appropriate ending to the tale of the scribe and his cursed quill," smiled the Great Sage. "I will let you read into it as you will."

The Cake and The Diamond

by Athyn Muendil

An alchemist tricks a thief!

I was in the Rat and the Pot, a foreigner cornerclub in Ald'ruhn, talking to my fellow Rats when I first saw the woman. Now, Breton women are fairly common in the Rat and the Pot. As a breed, they seem inclined to wander far from their perches in High Rock. Old Breton women, however, are not so migratory, and the wizened old biddy drew attention to herself, wandering about the room, talking to everyone.

Nimloth and Oediad were at their usual places, drinking their usual stuff. Oediad was showing off a prize he had picked up in some illicit manner — a colossal diamond, large as a baby's hand, and clear as spring water. I was admiring it when I heard the creaking of old bones behind me.

"Good day to you, friends," said the old woman. "My name is Abelle Chriditte, and I am in need of financial assistance to facilitate my transportation to Ald Redaynia."

"You'll want to see the Temple for charity," said Nimloth curtly.

"I am not looking for charity," said Abelle. "I'm looking to barter services."

"Don't make me sick, old woman," laughed Oediad.

"Did you say your name was Abelle Chriditte?" I asked, "Are you related to Abelle Chriditte, the High Rock alchemist?"

"Closely related," she said, with a cackle. "We are the same person. Perhaps I could prepare you a potion in exchange for gold? I noticed that you have in your possession a

very fine diamond. The magical qualities of diamonds are boundless."

"Sorry, old woman, I ain't giving it up for magic. It was trouble enough stealing this one," said Oediad. "I've got a fence who'll trade it for gold."

"But your fence will demand a certain percentage, will he not? What if I could give you a potion of invisibility in exchange? In return for that diamond, you could have the means to steal many more. A very fair exchange of services, I would say."

"It would be, but I have no gold to give you," said Oediad.

"I'll take what remains of the diamond after I've made the potion," said Abelle. "If you took it to the Mages Guild, you'd have to supply all the other ingredients and pay for it as well. But I learned my craft in the wild, where no Potion-makers existed to dissolve diamonds into dust. When you must do it all by hand, by simple skill, you are blessed with remnants those fool potion-makers at the Guild simply swallow up."

"That sounds all very nice," said Nimloth, "But how do we know your potion is going to work? If you make one potion, take the rest of Oediad's diamond, and leave, we won't know until you've gone whether the potion works or not."

"Ah, trust is so rare these days," sighed Abelle. "I suppose I could make two potions for you, and there'd still be a little bit of the diamond left for me. Not a lot, but perhaps enough to get me to Ald Redaynia. Then you could try the first potion right here and now, and see if you're satisfied or not."

"But," I interjected. "You could make one potion that works and one that doesn't, and take more of the diamond. She could even give you a slow-acting poison, and by the time she got to Ald Redaynia, you'd be dead."

"Bleedin' Kynareth, you Dunmer are suspicious! I will hardly have any diamond left, but I could make two potions of two doses each, so you can satisfy yourself that the potion works and has no negative effects. If you still don't trust me, come along with me to my table and witness my craft if you'd like."

So it was decided that I would accompany Abelle back to her table where she had all her traveling bags full of herbs and minerals, to make certain that she was not making two different potions. It took nearly an hour of preparation, but she kindly allowed me to finish her half-filled flagon of wine while I watched her work. Splintering the diamond and powdering the pieces required the bulk of the time; over and over again, she waved her gnarled hands over the gem, intoning ancient enchantments, breaking the facets of the stone into smaller and smaller pieces. Separately she made pastes of minced bittergreen, crushed red bulbs of dell'arco spae, and driblets of ciciliani oil. I finished the wine.

"Old woman," I finally said with a sigh. "How much longer is this going to take? I'm getting tired of watching you work."

"The Mages Guild has fooled the populace into thinking alchemy is a science," she said. "But if you're tired, rest your eyes."

My eyes closed, seemingly of their own volition. But there had been something in that wine. Something that made me do what she asked.

"I think I'll make up the potion as cakes. It's much more potent that way. Now, tell me, young man, what will your friends do once I give them the potion?"

"Mug you in the street afterwards to retrieve the rest of the diamond," I said simply. I didn't want to tell the truth, but there it was.

"I thought so, but I wanted to be certain. You may open your eyes now."

I opened my eyes. Abelle had made a small presentation on a wooden platter: two small cakes and a silver cutting knife.

"Pick up the cakes and bring them to the table," said Abelle. "And don't say anything, except to agree with whatever I say."

I did as I was told. It was a curious sensation. I didn't really mind being her puppet. Of course, in retrospect, I resent it, but it seemed perfectly natural at the time to obey without question.

Abelle handed the cakes to Oediad and I dutifully verified that both cakes were made the same way. She suggested that he cut one of the cakes in half, and she would take one piece and he'd take the other, just so he would know that they worked and weren't poisoned. Oediad thought it was a good idea, and used Abelle's knife to cut the cake. Abelle took the piece on the left and popped into her mouth. Oediad took the piece on the right and swallowed it more cautiously.

Abelle and all the bags she was carrying vanished from sight almost instantly. Nothing happened to Oediad.

"Why did it work for the witch and not for me?" cried Oediad.

"Because the diamond dust was only on the left-hand side of the blade," said the old alchemist through me. I felt her control lessening as the distance grew and she hurried invisibly down the dark Ald'ruhn street away from the Rat and the Pot.

We never found Abelle Chriditte or the diamond. Whether she completed her pilgrimage to Ald Redaynia is anyone's guess. The cakes had no effect, except to give Oediad a bad case of droops that lasted for nearly a week.

Fragment: On Artaeum

by Taurce il-Anselma

The Isle of Artaeum (ar-TAY-um) is the third largest island in the Summurset archipelago, located south of the Moridunon village of Potansa and west of the mainland village of Runcibae. It is best known for being home to the Psijic Order, perhaps the oldest monastic group in Tamriel.

The earliest written record of Psijics is from the 20th year of the First Era and tells the tale of the renowned Breton sage and author Voernet, traveling to the Isle of Artaeum to meet with Iachesis, the Ritemaster of the Psijics.

Even then, the Psijics were the counsellors of kings and proponents of the "Elder Way," taught to them by the original race that inhabited Tamriel. The Elder Way is a philosophy of meditation and study said to bind the forces of nature to the individual will. It differs from magicka in origin, but the effects are much the same.

That said, it is perhaps more than coincidence that the Isle of Artaeum literally vanished from the shores of Summurset at the beginning of the Second Era at about the time of the founding of the Mages Guild in Tamriel. Various historians and scholars have published theories about this, but perhaps none but Iachesis and his own could shed light on the matter.

Five hundred years passed and Artaeum returned. The Psijics on the Isle consisted of persons, mostly Elves, who had disappeared and were presumed dead in the Second Era. They could not or would not offer any explanation for Artaeum's whereabouts during that time, or the fate of Iachesis and the original council of Artaeum.

Currently, the Psijics are led by the Loremaster Celarus, who has presided over the Council of Artaeum for the last two hundred and fifty years. The Council's influence in Tamrielan politics is tidal. The kings of Sumurset, particularly those of Moridunon, have often sought the Psijics' opinion. Emperor Uriel V was much influenced by the Council in the early, most glorious parts of his reign, before his disastrous attack on Akavir. It has even been suggested that the fleet of King Orghum of Pyandonea was destroyed by a joint effort of Emperor Antiochus and the Psijic Order. The last four emperors, Uriel VI, Morihatha, Pelagius IV, and Uriel VII, have been suspicious of the Psijics enough to refuse ambassadors from the Isle of Artaeum within the Imperial City.

The Isle of Artaeum is difficult to chart geographically. It is said that it shifts continuously either at random or by decree of the Council. Visitors to the island are so rare as to be almost unheard of. Anyone desirous of a meeting with a Psijic may find contacts in Potansa and Runcibae as well as many of the kingdoms of Summurset.

Were it more accessible, Artaeum would be a favored destination for travelers. I have been to the Isle once and still dream of its idyllic orchards and clear pastures, its still and silent lagoons, its misty woodlands, and the unique Psijic architecture that seems to be as natural as its surroundings as well as wondrous in its own right. The Ceporah Tower in particular I would study, for it is a relic from a civilization that predates the High Elves by several hundred years and is still used in certain rites by the Psijics. Perhaps one day I might return.

Note: The author is currently on the Isle of Artaeum by gracious consent of Master Sargenius of the Council of Artaeum.

The Old Ways

by Celarus the Loremaster

We who know the Old Ways are well aware of the existence of a spiritual world invisible to the unenlightened. Just as one living in a kingdom but unaware of the political machinations underneath may see a new tax or battle preparation as the caprices of fortune, many observe floods, famines, and madness with helpless incomprehension. This is deplorable. As the great Cuilean Darnizhaan moaned, "The power of ignorance can shatter ebony like glass."

What, after all, is the origin of these spiritual forces that move the invisible strings of Mundus? Any neophyte of Artaeum knows that these spirits are our ancestors — and that, while living, they too were bewildered by the spirits of their ancestors, and so on back to the original Acharyai. The Daedra and gods to whom the common people turn are no more than the spirits of superior men and women whose power and passion granted them great influence in the afterworld.

Certainly this is our truth and our religion. But how does it help us in our sacred duty of seliffrnsae, or providing "grave and faithful counsel" to lesser men?

Primarily, it is easy to grasp the necessity both of endowing good men with great power and making powerful men good. We recognize the multiple threats that a strong tyrant represents — breeds cruelty which feeds the Daedra Boethiah and hatred which feeds the Daedra Vaermina; if he should die having performed a particularly malevolent act, he may go to rule in Oblivion; and worst of all, he inspires other villains to thirst after power and other rulers to embrace villainy. Knowing this, we have developed patience in our dealings with such despots. They should be crippled, humiliated, impoverished, imprisoned. Other counsellors may advocate assassination or warfare — which, aside from its spiritual insignificance, is expensive and likely to inflict at least as much pain on the innocents as the brutish dictator. No, we are intelligence gatherers, dignified diplomats — not revolutionaries.

How, then, are our counsellors "faithful"? We are faithful only to the Old Ways — it is essential always to remember the spiritual world while keeping our eyes open in the physical one. Performing the Rites of Moawita on the 2nd of Hearth Fire and the Vigyld on the 1st of Second Seed are essential means of empowering salutary spirits and debilitating unclean ones. How, then, are we at once faithful to those we counsel and to the Isle of Artaeum? Perhaps the sage Taheritae said it best: "In Mundus, conflict and disparity are what bring change, and change is the most sacred of the Eleven Forces. Change is the force without focus or origin. It is the duty of the disciplined Psijic ["Enlightened One"] to dilute change where it brings greed, gluttony, sloth, ignorance, prejudice, cruelty... [here Taheritae lists the rest of the 111 Prodigalities], and to encourage change where it brings excellence, beauty, happiness, and enlightenment.

As such, the faithful counsel has but one master: His mind. If the man the Psijic counsels acts wickedly and brings oegnithr ["bad change"] and will otherwise not be counselled, it is the Psijic's duty to counterbalance the oegnithr by any means necessary [emphasis mine]."

A student of the Old Ways may indeed ally himself to a lord — but it is a risky relationship. It cannot be stressed enough that the choice be wisely made. Should the lord refuse wise counsel and order the Psijic (to use Taheritae's outmoded word) to perform an act contrary to the teachings of the Old Ways, there are few available options. The Psijic may obey, albeit unwillingly, and fall prey to the dark forces against which he has devoted his life. The Psijic may abandon his lord, which will bring shame on him and the Isle of Artaeum, and so may never be allowed home again. Or the Psijic may simply kill himself.

An Accounting of the Elder Scrolls

by Quintus Nerevelus Former Imperial Librarian

After the supposed theft of an Elder Scroll from our Imperial Library, I endeavored to find any sort of index or catalogue of the Scrolls in our possession so that such situations may be avoided (or at least properly verified) in the future. To my dismay, I discovered that the Moth Priests are notoriously inexact when it comes to the actual physical manifestations of the Scrolls, and had no idea how many they held, or how they were organized. Merely asking the question evoked chuckles, as if a child was asking why dogs cannot talk.

I will confess, my jealousy of the ones who can read the Scrolls grows, but I am not yet willing to sacrifice my sight to alleged knowledge. The older Moth Priests I attempt to engage in conversation seem as batty as any other elder who has lost their mind, so I fail to see what wisdom is imparted from the reading.

In any case, I set out to create my own index of the Elder Scrolls, in cooperation with the monks. Day by day, we went through the tower halls, with them telling me the general nature of each Elder Scroll so that I might record its location. Always careful never to glimpse the writings myself, I had only their word to go on. I meticulously drew out a map of the chambers, where Scrolls relating to various specific prophecies were located, where particular periods of history were housed. In all, it took nearly a year of plodding, but at last I had rough notes on the entirety of the library to begin my collation.

It was here that things began to go amiss. In studying my notes, I found many areas of overlap and outright contradiction. In some cases different monks would claim the same scroll to be at opposite ends of the tower. I know they have no taste for jesting, or else I would suspect I was being made the fool in some game of theirs.

I spoke to one of the older monks to relate my concerns, and he hung his head in sorrow for my wasted time. "Did I not tell you," he coughed, "when you started this that all efforts would be futile? The Scrolls do not exist in countable form."

"I had thought you meant there were too many to be counted."

"There are, but that is not the least of their complexities. Turn to the repository behind you, and tell me how many Scrolls are locked therein."

I ran my fingers over the metal casings, tallying each rounded edge that they encountered. I turned back — "Fourteen," I said.

"Hand me the eighth one," he said, reaching out his hand.

I guided the cylinder into his palm, and he gave a slight nod to acknowledge it. "Now, count again."

Humoring him, I again passed my hands over the Scrolls, but could not believe what I was feeling.

"Now... now there are eighteen!" I gasped.

The old monk chuckled, his cheeks pushing up his blindfold until it folded over itself. "And in fact," he said, "there always were."

It was then that I enrolled as the oldest novice ever accepted into the Cult of the Ancestor Moth.

Effects of the Elder Scrolls

It is widely known among scholars that the Elder Scrolls entail a certain hazard in their very reading. The mechanism of the effects has, at present, been largely unknown — theories of hidden knowledge and divine retribution were the subject of idle speculation with little investigation.

I, Justinius Poluhnius, have undertaken to thoroughly document the ailments afflicted by the Elder Scrolls on their readers, though a unified theory of how they manifest continues to elude me and remains a subject for future study.

I have grouped the effects into four, finding that the avenue of experience depends largely upon the mind of the reader. If this is unclear, I hope that a proper dichotomy will lay it plain.

Group the First

For one who has received no training in the history or nature of the Elder Scrolls, the scroll itself is, effectively, inert. No prophecy can be scried nor knowledge obtained. While the scroll will not impart learning to the uninformed, nor will it afflict them in any adverse fashion. Visually, the scroll will appear to be awash in odd lettering and symbols. Those who know their astronomy often claim to recognize constellations in the patterns and connections, but such conjecture is impossible to further investigate since the very nature of this study necessitates unlearned subjects.

Group the Second: The Unguarded Intellects

It is this second group that realizes the greatest danger from attempting to read the scrolls. These are subjects who have an understanding of the nature of the Elder Scrolls and possess sufficient knowledge to actually read what is inscribed there. They have not, however, developed adequate discipline to stave off the mind-shattering effect of having a glimpse of infinity. These unfortunate souls are struck immediately, irrevocably, and completely blind. Such is the price for overreaching one's faculties. It bears mentioning, though, that with the blindness also comes a fragment of that hidden knowledge — whether the future, the past, or the deep natures of being is dependent on the individual and their place in the greater spheres. But the knowledge does come.

Group the Third: Mediated Understanding

Alone in Tamriel, it would appear that only the Cult of the Ancestor Moth has discovered the discipline to properly guard one's mind when reading the scrolls. Their novitiates must undergo the most rigorous mental cultivation, and they often spend a decade or more at the monastery before being allowed to read their first Elder Scroll. The monks say this is for the initiates' own protection, as they must have witnessed many Unguarded Intellects among their more eager ranks. With appropriate fortitude, these readers also receive blindness, though at a far lesser magnitude than the Unguarded. Their vision fogs slightly, but they retain shape, color, and enough acuity to continue to read mundane texts. The knowledge they gain from the scroll is also tempered somewhat — it requires stages of meditation and reflection to fully appreciate and express what one saw.

Group the Fourth: Illuminated Understanding

Between the previous group and this one exists a continuum that has, at present, only been traversed by the monks of the Ancestor Moth. With continued readings the monks become gradually more and more blind, but receive greater and more detailed knowledge. As they spend their waking hours pondering the revelations, they also receive a further degree of mental fortitude. There is, for every monk, a day of Penultimate Reading, when the only knowledge the Elder Scroll imparts is that the monk's next reading shall be his last.

For each monk the Penultimate Reading comes at a different and unknowable time — preliminary work has been done to predict the occurrence by charting the severity of an individual monk's blindness, but all who reach these later stages report that the increasing blindness seems to taper with increased readings. Some pose the notion that some other, unseen, sense is, in fact, continuing to diminish at this upper range, but I shall leave such postulations to philosophers.

To prepare for his Ultimate Reading, a monk typically withdraws to seclusion in order to reflect upon a lifetime of revelations and appoint his mind for reception of his last. Upon this final reading, he is forever blinded as sure as those Unguarded ones who raced to knowledge. The Illuminated one, though, has retained his understanding over a lifetime and typically possesses a more integral notion of what has been revealed to him.

It is hoped that this catalog will prove useful to those who wish to further our mortal understanding of the Elder Scrolls. The Moth priests remain aloof about these matters, taking the gradual debilitation that comes with reading as a point of pride. May this serve as a useful starting point for those hoping to take up such study.

Dictated to Anstius Metchim, 4th of Last Seed in the 126th year of the Second Era

N'Gasta! Kvata! Kvakis!

by N'Gasta

An obscure text written in the language of the Sload by a necromancer

An obscure text in the language of the Sload, purportedly written by the Second Era Western necromancer, N'Gasta.

N'Gasta! Kvata! Kvakis! ahkstas so novajxletero (oix jhemile) so Ranetauw. Ricevas gxin pagintaj membrauw kaj aliaj individuauw, kiujn iamaniere tusxas so raneta aktivado. En gxi aperas informauw unuavice pri so lokauw so cxiumonataj kunvenauw, sed nature ankoix pri aliaj aktuasoj aktivecauw so societo. Ne malofte enahkstas krome plej diversaspekta materialo eduka oix distra.

So interreta Kvako (retletera kaj verjheauw) ahkstas unufsonke alternativaj kanasouw por distribui so enhavon so papera Kva! Kvak!. Sed alifsonke so enhavauw so diversaj verjheauw antoixvible ne povas kaj ecx ne vus cxiam ahksti centprocente so sama. En malvaste cirkusonta paperfolio ekzemple ebsos publikigi ilustrajxauwn, kiuj pro kopirajtaj kiasouw ne ahkstas uzebsoj en so interreto. Alifsonke so masoltaj kostauw reta distribuo forigas so spacajn limigauwn kaj permahksas pli ampleksan enhavon, por ne paroli pri gxishora aktualeco.

Tiuj cirkonstancauw rahkspeguligxos en so aspekto so Kvakoa, kiu ja cetere servos ankoix kiel gxeneraso retejo so ranetauw.

Souls, Black and White

The nature of the soul is not knowable. Every wizard that has attempted it vanishes without a trace. What can be known is that souls are a source of mystic energy that can be harvested.

Every creature, living or dead, is powered by a soul. Without it, they are just lumps of flesh or piles of bones. This animating force can be contained within a soul gem, if the soul gem has the capacity. From the gem, the power can be used to power magical items.

Centuries of experimentation has demonstrated that there are black souls and white souls. Only the rare black soul gem can hold the soul of a higher creature, such as a man or an elf. While the souls of lesser creatures can be captured by gems of many colors, they are all categorized as white soul gems. Hence the division of souls into black and white.

White souls are far safer than black souls, although not as powerful. Beginning students of Mysticism should not dabble in black souls or black soul gems. Even if one were to ignore the guild strictures against the necromatic arts used to power black soul gems, it is dangerous to the caster to handle them for long. If the gem is not precisely the size of the encased soul, small bits of the caster's soul may leak into the gem when it is touched.

The Book of Life and Service

Book relating to the undead of the Soul Cairn

The Ranks of the Blessed:

Blessed are the Bonemen, for they serve without
self in spirit forever.

Blessed are the Mistmen, for they blend in the glory
of the transcendent spirit.

Blessed are the Wrathmen, for they render their
rage unto the ages.

Blessed are the Masters, for they bridge the past
and span the future.

The Litany of Service:

The Boneman's Oath

We die.
We pray.
To live.
We serve.

The Master's Voice

You swore.
To Serve.
Your Lord.

The Monomyth

"In Mundus, conflict and disparity are what bring change, and change is the most sacred of the Eleven Forces. Change is the force without focus or origin."– Oegnithr, Taheritae, Psijic Order.

Simply put, the schism in the Human/Aldmeri worldview is the mortal's relationship to the divine. Humans take the humble path that they were created by the immortal forces, while the Aldmer claim descent from them. It doesn't seem like much, but it is a distinction that colors the rest of their diverging mythologies.

All Tamrielic religions begin the same. Man or mer, things begin with the dualism of Anu and His Other. These twin forces go by many names: Anu-Padomay, Anuiel–Sithis, Ak–El, Satak–Akel, Is–Is Not. Anuiel is the Everlasting Ineffable Light, Sithis is the Corrupting Inexpressible Action. In the middle is the Gray Maybe ('Nirn' in the Ehlnofex).

In most cultures, Anuiel is honored for his part of the interplay that creates the world, but Sithis is held in highest esteem because he's the one that causes the reaction. Sithis is thus the Original Creator, an entity who intrinsically causes change without design. Even the hist acknowledge this being.

Anuiel is also perceived of as Order, opposed to the Sithis–Chaos. Perhaps it is easier for mortals to envision change than perfect stasis, for often Anuiel is relegated to the mythic background of Sithis' fancies. In Yokudan folk–tales, which are among the most vivid in the world, Satak is only referred to a handful of times, as "the Hum"; he is a force so prevalent as to be not really there at all.

In any case, from these two beings spring the et'Ada, or Original Spirits. To humans these et'Ada are the Gods and Demons; to the Aldmer, the Aedra/Daedra, or the 'Ancestors'. All of the Tamrielic pantheons fill their rosters from these et'Ada, though divine membership often differs from culture to culture. Like Anu and Padomay, though, every one of these pantheons contains the archetypes of the Dragon God and the Missing God.

The Dragon God and the Missing God

The Dragon God is always related to Time, and is universally revered as the "First God." He is often called Akatosh, "whose perch from Eternity allowed the day." He is the central God of the Cyrodilic Empire.

The Missing God is always related to the Mortal Plane, and is a key figure in the Human/Aldmeri schism. The 'missing' refers to either his palpable absence from the pantheon (another mental distress that is interpreted a variety of ways), or the removal of his 'divine spark' by the other immortals. He is often called Lorkhan, and his epitaphs are many, equally damnable and devout.

Note that Tamriel and the Mortal Plane do not exist yet. The Gray Maybe is still the playground of the Original Spirits. Some are more bound to Anu's light, others to the unknowable void. Their constant flux and interplay increase their number, and their personalities take long to congeal. When Akatosh forms, Time begins, and it becomes easier for some spirits to realize themselves as beings with a past and a future. The strongest of the recognizable spirits crystallize: Mephala, Arkay, Yffre, Magnus, Rupgta, etc., etc. Others remain as concepts, ideas, or emotions. One of the strongest of these, a barely formed urge that the others call Lorkhan, details a plan to create Mundus, the Mortal Plane.

Humans, with the exception of the Redguards, see this act as a divine mercy, an enlightenment whereby lesser creatures can reach immortality. Aldmer, with the exception of the Dark Elves, see this act as a cruel deception, a trick that sundered their connection to the spirit plane.

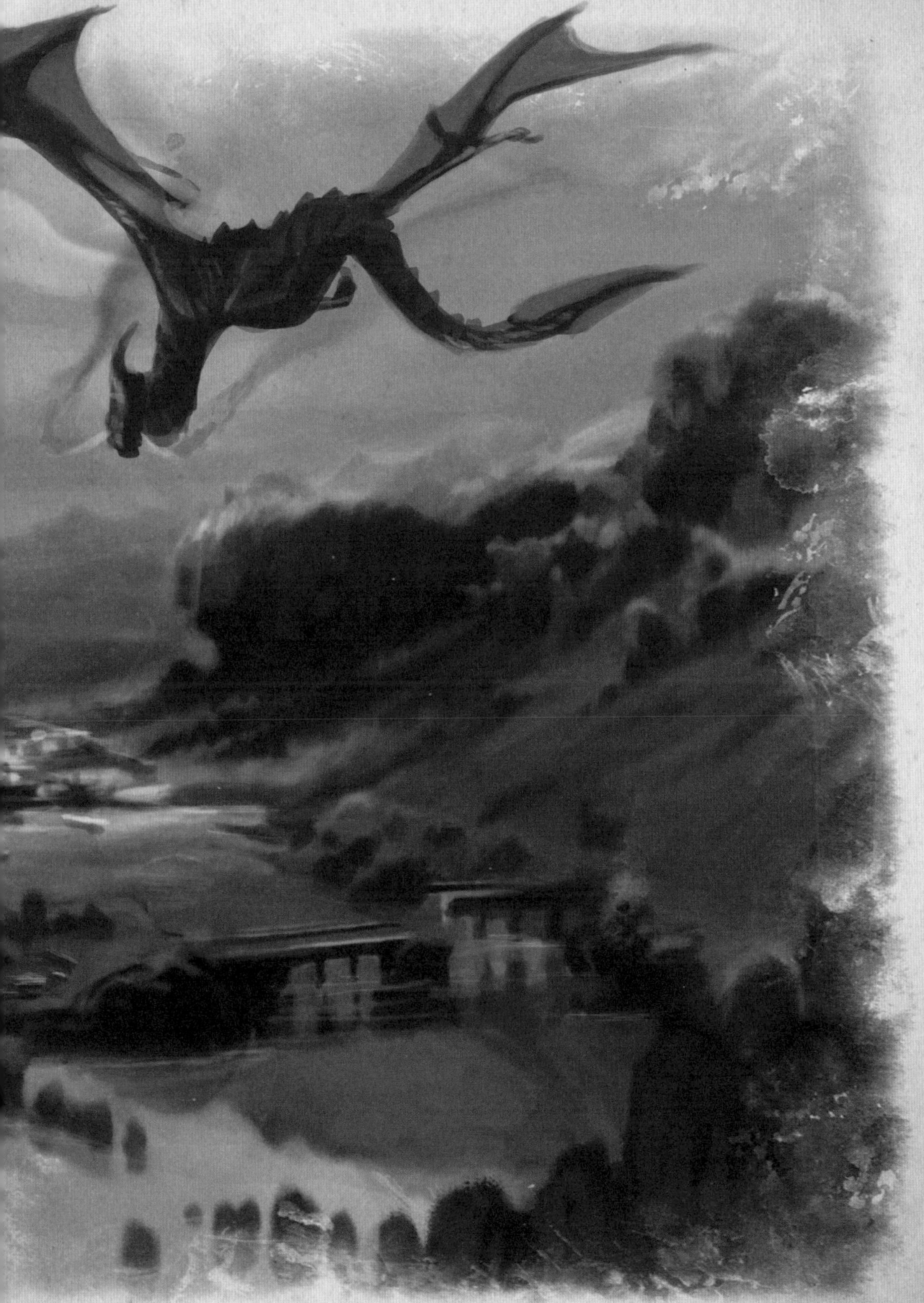

The Myth of Aurbis

Subtitled "The Psijiic Compensation," "Mythic Aurbis" was an attempt by Artaeum apologists to explain the basics of Aldmeri religion to Uriel V in the early, glorious part of his reign. It quietly avoided any blame or bias against the Lorkhan-concept, which was still held in esteem by the Cyrodiils as "Shezarr", the missing sibling of the Divines. Despite this, the Psijiici still give a nice summary of the Elder view, and it will serve our purposes here. This version comes from the archives of the Imperial Seminary from the handwritten notes of an unknown scribe.

Mythic Aurbis exists, and has existed from time without measure, as a fanciful Unnatural Realm.

'Aurbis' is used to connote the imperceptible Penumbra, the Gray Center between the IS/IS NOT of Anu and Padomay. It contains the multitude realms of Aetherius and Oblivion, as well as other, less structured forms.

The magical beings of Mythic Aurbis live for a long time and have complex narrative lives, creating the patterns of myth.

These are spirits made from bits of the immortal polarity. The first of these was Akatosh the Time Dragon, whose formation made it easier for other spirits to structure themselves. Gods and demons form and reform and procreate.

Finally, the magical beings of Mythic Aurbis told the ultimate story — that of their own death. For some this was an artistic transfiguration into the concrete, non-magical substance of the world. For others, this was a war in which all were slain, their bodies becoming the substance of the world. For yet others, this was a romantic marriage and parenthood, with the parent spirits naturally having to die and give way to the succeeding mortal races.

The agent of this communal decision was Lorkhan, whom most early myths vilify as a trickster or deceiver. More sympathetic versions of this story point out Lorkhan as being the reason the mortal plane exists at all.

The magical beings created the races of the mortal Aurbis in their own image, either consciously as artists and craftsmen, or as the fecund rotting matter out of which the mortals sprung forth, or in a variety of other analogical senses.

The magical beings, then, having died, became the et'Ada. The et'Ada are the things perceived and revered by the mortals as gods, spirits, or geniuses of Aurbis. Through their deaths, these magical beings separated themselves in nature from the other magical beings of the Unnatural realms.

The Daedra were created at this time also, being spirits and Gods more attuned to Oblivion, or that realm closer to the Void of Padomay. This act is the dawn of the Mythic (Merethic) Era. It has been perceived by the earliest mortals many different ways, either as a joyous 'second creation', or (especially by the Elves) as a painful fracturing from the divine. The originator of the event is always Lorkhan.

Lorkhan

This Creator-Trickster-Tester deity is in every Tamrielic mythic tradition. His most popular name is the Aldmeri "Lorkhan," or Doom Drum. He convinced or contrived the Original Spirits to bring about the creation of the Mortal Plane, upsetting the status quo much like his father Padomay had introduced instability into the universe in the Beginning Place. After the world is materialized, Lorkhan is separated from his divine center, sometimes involuntarily, and wanders the creation of the et'Ada. Interpretations of these events differ widely by culture. Below are some of the better known.

Yokudan, "Satakal the Worldskin"

"Satak was First Serpent, the Snake who came Before, and all the worlds to come rested in the glimmer of its scales. But it was so big there was nothing but, and thus it was coiled around and around itself, and the worlds to come slid across each other but none had room to breathe or even be. And so the worlds called to something to save them, to let them out, but of course there was nothing outside the First Serpent, so aid had to come from inside it; this was Akel, the Hungry Stomach. Akel made itself known, and Satak could only think about what it was, and it was the best hunger, so it ate and ate. Soon there was enough room to live in the worlds and things began. These things were new and they often made mistakes, for there was hardly time to practice being things before. So most things ended quickly or were not good or gave up on themselves. Some things were about to start, but they were eaten up as Satak got to that part of its body. This was a violent time.

"Pretty soon Akel caused Satak to bite its own heart and that was the end. The hunger, though, refused to stop, even in death, and so the First Serpent shed its skin to begin anew. As the old world died, Satakal began, and when things realized this pattern so did they realize what their part in it was. They began to take names, like Ruptga or Tuwhacca, and they strode about looking for their kin. As Satakal ate itself over and over, the strongest spirits learned to bypass the cycle by moving at strange angles. They called this process the Walkabout, a way of striding between the worldskins. Ruptga was so big that he was able to place the stars in the sky so that weaker spirits might find their way easier. This practice became so easy for the spirits that it became a place, called the Far Shores, a time of waiting until the next skin.

"Ruptga was able to sire many children through the cycles and so he became known as the Tall Papa. He continued to place stars to map out the void for others, but after so many cycles there were almost too many spirits to help out. He made himself a helper from the detritus of past skins and this was Sep, or Second Serpent. Sep had much of the Hungry Stomach still left in him, multiple hungers from multiple skins. He was so hungry he could not think straight. Sometimes he would just eat the spirits he was supposed to help, but Tall Papa would always reach in and take them back out. Finally, tired of helping Tall Papa, Sep went and gathered the rest of the old skins and balled them up, tricking spirits to help him, promising them this was how you reached the new world, by making one out of the old. These spirits loved this way of living, as it was easier. No more jumping from place to place. Many spirits joined in, believing this was good thinking. Tall Papa just shook his head.

"Pretty soon the spirits on the skin-ball started to die, because they were very far from the real world of Satakal. And they found that it was too far to jump into the Far Shores now. The spirits that were left pleaded with Tall Papa to take them back. But grim Ruptga would not, and he told the spirits that they must learn new ways to follow the stars to the Far Shores now. If they could not, then they must live on through their children, which was not the same as before. Sep, however, needed more punishment, and so Tall Papa squashed the Snake with a big stick. The hunger fell out of Sep's dead mouth and was the only thing left of the Second Serpent. While the rest of the new world was allowed to strive back to godhood, Sep could only slink around in a dead skin, or swim about in the sky, a hungry void that jealously tried to eat the stars."

Cyrodiilic "Shezarr's Song"

"This was a new thing that Shezarr described to the Gods, becoming mothers and fathers, being responsible, and making great sacrifices, with no guarantee of success, but Shezarr spoke beautifully to them, and moved them beyond mystery and tears. Thus the Aedra gave free birth to the world, the beasts, and the beings, making these things from parts of themselves. This free birth was very painful, and afterwards the Aedra were no longer young, and strong, and powerful, as they had been from the beginning of days.

"Some Aedra were disappointed and bitter in their loss, and angry with Shezarr, and with all creation, for they felt Shezarr had lied and tricked them. These Aedra, the Gods of the Aldmer, led by Auri-El, were disgusted by their enfeebled selves, and by what they had created. 'Everything is spoiled, for now, and for all time, and the most we can do is teach the Elven Races to suffer nobly, with dignity, and chastise ourselves for our folly, and avenge ourselves upon Shezarr and his allies.' Thus are the Gods of the Elves dark and brooding, and thus are the Elves ever dissatisfied with mortality, and always proud and stoic despite the harshness of this cruel and indifferent world.

"Other Aedra looked upon creation, and were well pleased. These Aedra, the Gods of Men and Beast Folk, led by Akatosh, praised and cherished their wards, the Mortal Races. 'We have suffered, and are diminished, for all time, but the mortal world we have made is glorious, filling our hearts and spirits with hope. Let us teach the Mortal Races to live well, to cherish beauty and honor, and to love one another as we love them.' Thus are the Gods of Men tender and patient, and thus are Men and Beast Folk great in heart for joy or suffering, and ambitious for greater wisdom and a better world.

"Now when the Daedra Lords heard Shezarr, they mocked him, and the other Aedra,

'Cut parts of ourselves off? And lose them? Forever? That's stupid! You'll be sorry! We are far smarter than you, for we will create a new world out of ourselves, but we will not cut it off, or let it mock us, but we will make this world within ourselves, forever ours, and under our complete control.'

"So the Daedra Lords created the Daedric Realms, and all the ranks of Lesser Daedra, great and small. And, for the most part, the Daedra Lords were well pleased with this arrangement, for they always had worshippers and servants and playthings close to hand. But, at the same time, they sometimes looked with envy upon the Mortal Realms, for though mortals were foul and feeble and contemptible, their passions and ambitions were also far more surprising and entertaining than the antics of the Lesser Daedra. Thus do the Daedra Lords court and seduce certain amusing specimens of the Mortal Races, especially the passionate and powerful. It gives the Daedra Lords special pleasure to steal away from Shezarr and the Aedra the greatest and most ambitious mortals. 'Not only are you fools to mutilate yourselves,' gloat the Daedra Lords, 'But you cannot even keep the best pieces, which prefer the glory and power of the Daedra Lords to the feeble vulgarity of the mush-minded Aedra.'"

Altmeri "The Heart of the World"

"Anu encompa ssed, and encompasses, all things. So that he might know himself he created Anuiel, his soul and the soul of all things. Anuiel, as all souls, was given to self-reflection, and for this he needed to differentiate between his forms, attributes, and intellects. Thus was born Sithis, who was the sum of all the limitations Anuiel would utilize to ponder himself. Anuiel, who was the soul of all things, therefore became many things, and this interplay was and is the Aurbis.

"At first the Aurbis was turbulent and confusing, as Anuiel's ruminations went on without design. Aspects of the Aurbis then asked for a schedule to follow or procedures whereby they might enjoy themselves a little longer outside of perfect knowledge. So that he might know himself this way, too, Anu created Auriel, the soul of his soul. Auriel bled through the Aurbis as a new force, called time. With time, various aspects of the Aurbis began to understand their natures and limitations. They took names, like Magnus or Mara or Xen. One of these, Lorkhan, was more of a limit than a nature, so he could never last long anywhere.

"As he entered every aspect of Anuiel, Lorkhan would plant an idea that was almost wholly based on limitation. He outlined a plan to create a soul for the Aurbis, a place where the aspects of aspects might even be allowed to self-reflect. He gained many followers; even Auriel, when told he would become the king of the new world, agreed to help Lorkhan. So they created the Mundus, where their own aspects might live, and became the et'Ada.

"But this was a trick. As Lorkhan knew, this world contained more limitations than not and was therefore hardly a thing of Anu at all. Mundus was the House of Sithis. As their aspects began to die off, many of the et'Ada vanished completely. Some escaped, like Magnus, and that is why there are no limitations to magic. Others, like Y'ffre, transformed themselves into the Ehlnofey, the Earthbones, so that the whole world might not die. Some had to marry and make children just to last. Each generation was weaker than the last, and soon there were Aldmer. Darkness caved in. Lorkhan made armies out of the weakest souls and named them Men, and they brought Sithis into every quarter.

"Auriel pleaded with Anu to take them back, but he had already filled their places with something else. But his soul was gentler and granted Auriel his Bow and Shield, so that he might save the Aldmer from the hordes of Men. Some had already fallen, like the Chimer, who listened to tainted et'Ada, and others, like the Bosmer, had soiled Time's line by taking Mannish wives.

"Auriel could not save Altmora, the Elder Wood, and it was lost to Men. They were chased south and east to Old Ehlnofey, and Lorkhan was close behind. He shattered that land into many. Finally Trinimac, Auriel's greatest knight, knocked Lorkhan down in front of his army and reached in with more than hands to take his Heart. He was undone. The Men dragged Lorkhan's body away and swore blood vengeance on the heirs of Auriel for all time.

"But when Trinimac and Auriel tried to destroy the Heart of Lorkhan it laughed at them. It said, "This Heart is the heart of the world, for one was made to satisfy the other." So Auriel fastened the thing to an arrow and let it fly long into the sea, where no aspect of the new world may ever find it."

A Children's Anuad: The Paraphrased

The first ones were brothers: Anu and Padomay. They came into the Void, and Time began.

As Anu and Padomay wandered the Void, the interplay of Light and Darkness created Nir. Both Anu and Padomay were amazed and delighted with her appearance, but she loved Anu, and Padomay retreated from them in bitterness.

Nir became pregnant, but before she gave birth, Padomay returned, professing his love for Nir. She told him that she loved only Anu, and Padomay beat her in rage. Anu returned, fought Padomay, and cast him outside Time. Nir gave birth to Creation, but died from her injuries soon after. Anu, grieving, hid himself in the sun and slept.

Meanwhile, life sprang up on the twelve worlds of creation and flourished. After many ages, Padomay was able to return to Time. He saw Creation and hated it. He swung his sword, shattering the twelve worlds in their alignment. Anu awoke, and fought Padomay again. The long and furious battle ended with Anu the victor. He cast aside the body of his brother, who he believed was dead, and attempted to save Creation by forming the remnants of the 12 worlds into one — Nirn, the world of Tamriel. As he was doing so, Padomay struck him through the chest with one last blow. Anu grappled with his brother and pulled them both outside of Time forever.

The blood of Padomay became the Daedra. The blood of Anu became the stars. The mingled blood of both became the Aedra (hence their capacity for good and evil, and their greater affinity for earthly affairs than the Daedra, who have no connection to Creation).

On the world of Nirn, all was chaos. The only survivors of the twelve worlds of Creation were the Ehlnofey and the Hist. The Ehlnofey are the ancestors of Mer and Men. The Hist are the trees of Argonia. Nirn originally was all land, with interspersed seas, but no oceans.

A large fragment of the Ehlnofey world landed on Nirn relatively intact, and the Ehlnofey living there were the ancestors of the Mer. These Ehlnofey fortified their borders from the chaos outside, hid their pocket of calm, and attempted to live on as before. Other Ehlnofey arrived on Nirn scattered amid the confused jumble of the shattered worlds, wandering and finding each other over the years. Eventually, the wandering Ehlnofey found the hidden land of Old Ehlnofey, and were amazed and joyful to find their kin living amid the splendor of ages past. The wandering Ehlnofey expected to be welcomed into the peaceful realm, but the Old Ehlnofey looked on them as degenerates, fallen from their former glory. For whatever reason, war broke out, and raged across the whole of Nirn. The Old Ehlnofey retained their ancient power and knowledge, but the Wanderers were more numerous, and toughened by their long struggle to survive on

Nirn. This war reshaped the face of Nirn, sinking much of the land beneath new oceans, and leaving the lands as we know them (Tamriel, Akavir, Atmora, and Yokuda). The Old Ehlnofey realm, although ruined, became Tamriel. The remnants of the Wanderers were left divided on the other 3 continents.

Over many years, the Ehlnofey of Tamriel became: — the Mer (elves), — the Dwemer (the Deep Ones, sometimes called dwarves), — the Chimer (the Changed Ones, who later became the Dunmer), — the Dunmer (the Dark or Cursed Ones, the dark elves), — the Bosmer (the Green or Forest Ones, the wood elves), and — the Altmer (The Elder or High Ones, the high elves).

On the other continents, the Wandering Ehlnofey became the Men — the Nords of Atmora, the Redguards of Yokuda, and the Tsaesci of Akavir.

The Hist were bystanders in the Ehlnofey war, but most of their realm was destroyed as the war passed over it. A small corner of it survived to become Black Marsh in Tamriel, but most of their realm was sunk beneath the sea.

Eventually, Men returned to Tamriel. The Nords were the first, colonizing the northern coast of Tamriel before recorded history, led by the legendary Ysgramor. The thirteenth of his line, King Harald, was the first to appear in written history. And so the Mythic Era ended.

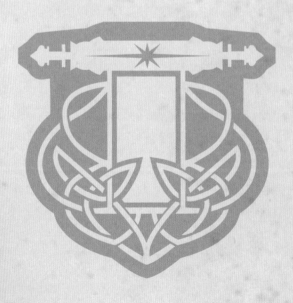

An Overview Of Gods and Worship In Tamriel

by Brother Hetchfeld

Editor's Note: Brother Hetchfeld is an Associate Scribe at the Imperial University, Office of Introductory Studies.

Gods are commonly judged upon the evidence of their interest in worldly matters. A central belief in the active participation of Deities in mundane matters can be challenged by the reference to apparent apathy and indifference on the part of Gods during times of plague or famine.

From intervention in legendary quests to manifestations in common daily life, no pattern for the Gods of Tamriel activities is readily perceived. The concerns of Gods in many ways may seem unrelated or at best unconcerned with the daily trials of the mortal realm. The exceptions do exist, however.

Many historical records and legends point to the direct intervention of one or more gods at times of great need. Many heroic tales recount blessings of the divinity bestowed upon heroic figures who worked or quested for the good of a Deity or the Deity's temple. Some of the more powerful artifacts in the known world were originally bestowed upon their owners through such reward. It has also been reported that priests of high ranking in their temples may on occasion call upon their Deity for blessings or help in time of need. The exact nature of such contact and the blessings bestowed is given to much speculation, as the temples hold such associations secret and holy. This direct contact gives weight to the belief that the Gods are aware of the mortal realm. In many circumstances, however, these same Gods will do nothing in the face of suffering and death, seeming to feel no need to interfere. It is thus possible to conclude that we, as mortals, may not be capable of understanding more than a small fraction of the reasoning and logic such beings use.

One defining characteristic of all Gods and Goddesses is their interest in worship and deeds. Deeds in the form of holy quests are just one of the many things that bring the attention of a Deity. Deeds in everyday life, by conforming to the statutes and obligations of individual temples are commonly supposed to please a Deity. Performance of ceremony in a temple may also bring a Deity's attention. Ceremonies vary according to the individual Deity. The results are not always apparent but sacrifice and offerings are usually required to have any hope of gaining a Deity's attention.

While direct intervention in daily temple life has been recorded, the exact nature of the presence of a God in daily mundane life is a subject of controversy. A traditional saying of the Wood Elves is that "One man's miracle is another man's accident." While some gods are believed to take an active part of daily life, others are well known for their lack of interest in temporal affairs.

It has been theorized that gods do in fact gain strength from such things as worship through praise, sacrifice and deed. It may even be theorized that the number of worshippers a given Deity has may reflect on His overall position among the other Gods. This my own conjecture, garnered from the apparent ability of the larger temples to attain blessings and assistance from their God with greater ease than smaller religious institutions.

There are reports of the existence of spirits in our world that have the same capacity to use the actions and deeds of mortals to strengthen themselves as do the Gods. The understanding of the exact nature of such creatures would allow us to understand with more clarity the connection between a Deity and the Deity's worshipers.

The implication of the existence of such spirits leads to the speculation that these spirits may even be capable of raising themselves to the level of a God or Goddess. Motusuo of the Imperial Seminary has suggested that these spirits may be the remains of Gods and Goddesses who through time lost all or most of their following, reverting to their earliest most basic form. Practioners of the Old Ways say that there are no Gods, just greater and lesser spirits. Perhaps it is possible for all three theories to be true.

Varieties of Faith in the Empire

by Brother Mikhael Karkuxor of the Imperial College

This is my best attempt at a listing of the pantheons and associated divine spirits of Tamriel's dominant cultures. This list is by no means complete (the Imperial City of Cyrodiil alone boasts a vast host of saints and holy spirits). It only includes the most important spirits revered by native members of the culture. Other et'Ada, especially Daedra, are often familiar known to many cultures, though specific names are included here only when they possess a particular cultural significance. The omission of any reference to the worships of the Argonians of Black Marsh is a result of my complete inadequacy in reconciling the obscure and contradictory accounts available to me on that subject.

THE EIGHT PANTHEONS

CYRODIIL: Akatosh, Dibella, Arkay, Zenithar, Mara, Stendarr, Kynareth, Julianos, Shezarr, Tiber Septim, Morihaus, Reman

SKYRIM: Alduin, Dibella, Orkey, Tsun, Mara, Stuhn, Kyne, Jhunal, Shor, Ysmir, Herma-Mora, Maloch

ALTMER: Auri-El, Trinimac, Magnus, Syrabane, Yffre, Xarxes, Mara, Stendarr, Lorkhan, Phynaster

BOSMER: Auri-El, Yffre, Arkay, Z'en, Xarxes, Baan Dar, Mara, Stendarr, Lorkhan, Herma-Mora, Jone, Jode

DUNMER: Almalexia, Vivec, Sotha Sil, Boethiah, Mephala, Azura, Lorkhan, Nerevar, Molag Bal, Malacath, Sheogorath, Mehrunes Dagon

YOKUDA: Satakal, Ruptga, Tu'whacca, Zeht, Morwha, Tava, Malooc, Diagna, Sep, HoonDing, Leki, Onsi,

BRETONY: Akatosh, Magnus, Yffre, Dibella, Arkay, Zenithar, Mara, Stendarr, Kynareth, Julianos, Sheor, Phynaster

ELSWEYR: Alkosh, Khenarthi, Riddle'Thar, ja-Kha'jay, Mara, S'rendarr, Lorkhaj, Rajhin, Baan Dar, Azurah, Sheggorath

NOTES ON THE DIVINE SPIRITS OF THE PANTHEONS

Akatosh (Dragon God of Time): Akatosh is the chief deity of the Nine Divines (the major religious cult of Cyrodiil and its provinces), and one of two deities found in every Tamrielic religion (the other is Lorkhan). He is generally considered to be the first of the Gods to form in the Beginning Place; after his establishment, other spirits found the process of being easier and the various pantheons of the world emerged. He is the ultimate God of the Cyrodilic Empire, where he embodies the qualities of endurance, invincibility, and everlasting legitimacy.

Alduin (World Eater): Alduin is the Nordic variation of Akatosh, and only superficially resembles his counterpart in the Nine Divines. For example, Alduin's sobriquet, 'the world eater', comes from myths that depict him as the horrible, ravaging firestorm that destroyed the last world to begin this one. Nords therefore see the god of time as both creator and harbinger of the apocalypse. He is not the chief of the Nordic pantheon (in fact, that pantheon has no chief; see Shor, below) but its wellspring, albeit a grim and frightening one.

Alkosh (Dragon King of Cats): Pre-ri'Datta Dynasty Anaquinine deity. A variation on the Altmeri Auri-El, and thus an Akatosh-as-culture-hero for the earliest Khajiiti. His worship was co-opted during the establishment of the Riddle-T'har, and he still enjoys immense popularity in Elsweyr's wasteland regions. He is depicted as a fearsome dragon, a creature the Khajiit say 'is just a real big cat'. He repelled an early Aldmeri pogrom of Pelinal Whitestrake during mythic times.

Almalexia (Mother Morrowind): Most traces of Akatosh disappeared from ancient Chimer legends during their so-called 'exodus', primarily due to that god's association and esteem with the Altmeri. However, most aspects of Akatosh which seem so important to the mortal races, namely immortality, historicity, and genealogy, have conveniently resurfaced in Almalexia, the most popular of Morrowind's divine Tribunal.

Arkay (God of the Cycle of Life and Death): Member of the Nine Divines pantheon, and popular elsewhere as well. Arkay is often more important in those cultures where his father, Akatosh, is either less related to time or where his time aspects are difficult to comprehend by the layman. He is the god of burials and funeral rites, and is sometimes associated with the seasons. His priests are staunch opponents of necromancy and all forms of the undead. It is said that Arkay did not exist before the world was created by the gods under Lorkhan's supervision/urging/trickery. Therefore, he is sometimes called the Mortals' God.

Auri-El (King of the Aldmer): The Elven Akatosh is Auri-El. Auri-El is the soul of Anui-El, who, in turn, is the soul of Anu the Everything. He is the chief of most Aldmeri pantheons. Most Altmeri and Bosmeri claim direct descent from Auri-El. In his only known moment of weakness, he agreed to take his part in the creation of the mortal plane, that act which forever sundered the Elves from the spirit worlds of eternity. To make up for it, Auri-El led the original Aldmer against the armies of Lorkhan in mythic times, vanquishing that tyrant and establishing the first kingdoms of the Altmer, Altmora and Old Ehlnofey. He then ascended to heaven in full observance of his followers so that they might learn the steps needed to escape the mortal plane.

Azura (Goddess of Dusk and Dawn): Azura was the god-ancestor that taught the Chimer the mysteries needed to be different than the Altmer. Some of her more conventional teachings are sometimes attributed to Boethiah. In the stories, Azura is often more a communal cosmic force for the race as a whole than an ancestor or a god. Also known as the Anticipation of Sotha Sil. In Elsweyr, Azurah is nearly a wholly separate entity, yet she is still tied into the origins of Khajiiti out of Altmeri stock.

Baan Dar (The Bandit God): In most regions, Baan Dar is a marginal diety, a trickster spirit of thieves and beggars. In Elsweyr he is more important, and is regarded as the Pariah. In this aspect, Baan Dar becomes the cleverness or desperate genius of the long-suffering Khajiit, whose last minute plans always upset the machinations of their (Elven or Human) enemies.

Boethiah (Prince of Plots): Heralded by the Prophet Veloth, Boethiah is the original god-ancestor of the Dark Elves. Through his illuminations, the eventual 'Chimer', or Changed Folk, renounced all ties to the Aldmer and founded a new nation based on Daedric principles. All manner of Dark Elven cultural 'advances' are attributed to Boethiah, from philosophy to magic to 'responsible' architecture. Ancient Velothi allegories are uniformly heroic successes of Boethiah over enemies of every type, foundation stories of Chimeri struggle. Also known as the Anticipation of Almalexia.

Diagna (Orichalc God of the Sideways Blade): Hoary thuggish cult of the Redguards. Originated in Yokuda during the Twenty Seven Snake Folk Slaughter. Diagna was an avatar of the HoonDing (the Yokudan God of Make Way, see below) that achieved permanence. He was instrumental to the defeat of the Lefthanded Elves, as he brought orichalc weapons to the Yokudan people to win the fight. In Tamriel, he led a very tight knit group of followers against the Orcs of Orsinium during the height of their ancient power, but then faded into obscurity. He is now little more than a local power spirit of the Dragontail mountains.

Dibella (Goddess of Beauty): Popular god of the Nine Divines. In Cyrodiil, she has nearly a dozen different cults, some devoted to women, some to artists and aesthetics, and others to erotic instruction.

Herma-Mora (The Woodland Man): Ancient Atmoran demon who, at one time, nearly seduced the Nords into becoming Aldmer. Most Ysgramor myths are about escaping the wiles of old Herma-Mora. Also called the Demon of Knowledge, he is vaguely related to the cult origins of the Morag Tong ('Foresters Guild'), if only by association with his brother/sister, Mephala.

HoonDing (The Make Way God): Yokudan spirit of 'perseverance over infidels'. The HoonDing has historically materialized whenever the Redguards need to 'make way' for their people. In Tamrielic history this has only happened three times — twice in the first era during the Ra Gada invasion and once during the Tiber War. In this last incarnation, the HoonDing was said to have been either a sword or a crown, or both.

Jhunal (Rune God): The Nordic god of hermetic orders. After falling out of favor with the rest of that pantheon, he became Julianos of the Nine Divines. He is absent in modern Skyrim mythology.

Jode (Big Moon God): Aldmeri god of the Big Moon. Also called Masser or Mara's Tear. In Khajiiti religion, Jode is only one aspect of the Lunar Lattice, or ja-Kha'jay.

Jone (Little Moon God): Aldmeri god of the Little Moon. Also called Secunda or Stendarr's Sorrow. In Khajiiti religion, Jone is only one aspect of the Lunar Lattice, or ja-Kha'jay.

Julianos (God of Wisdom and Logic): Often associated with Jhunal, the Nordic father of language and mathematics, Julianos is the Cyrodilic god of literature, law, history, and contradiction. Monastic orders founded by Tiber Septim and dedicated to Julianos are the keepers of the Elder Scrolls.

Kyne (Kiss At the End): Nordic Goddess of the Storm. Widow of Shor and favored god of warriors. She is often called the Mother of Men. Her daughters taught the first Nords the use of the thu'um, or Storm Voice.

Kynareth (Goddess of Air): Kynareth is a member of the Nine Divines, the strongest of the Sky spirits. In some legends, she is the first to agree to Lorkhan's plan to invent the mortal plane, and provides the space for its creation in the void. She is also associated with rain, a phenomenon said not to occur before the removal of Lorkhan's divine spark.

Leki (Saint of the Spirit Sword): Goddess daughter of Tall Papa, Leki is the goddess of aberrant swordsmanship. The Na-Totambu of Yokuda warred to a standstill during the mythic era to decide who would lead the charge against the Lefthanded Elves. Their swordmasters, though, were so skilled in the Best Known Cuts as to be matched evenly. Leki introduced the Ephemeral Feint. Afterwards, a victor emerged and the war with the Aldmer began.

Lorkhan (The Missing God): This Creator-Trickster-Tester deity is in every Tamrielic mythic tradition. His most popular name is the Aldmeri 'Lorkhan', or Doom Drum. He convinced or contrived the Original Spirits to bring about the creation of the mortal plane, upsetting the status quo — much like his father Padomay had introduced instability into the universe in the Beginning Place. After the world is materialized, Lorkhan is separated from his divine center, sometimes involuntarily, and wanders the creation of the et'Ada. He and his metaphysical placement in the 'scheme of things' is interpreted a variety of ways. In Morrowind, for example, he is a being related to the Psijiic Endeavor, a process by which mortals are charged with transcending the gods that created them. To the High Elves, he is the most unholy of all higher powers, as he forever broke their connection to the spirit plane. In the legends, he is almost always an enemy of the Aldmer and, therefore, a hero of early Mankind.

Lorkhaj (Moon Beast): Pre-ri'Datta Dynasty Anaquinine deity, easily identified with the Missing God, Lorkhan.

Magnus (Magus): The god of sorcery, Magnus withdrew from the creation of the world at the last second, though it cost him dearly. What is left of him on the world is felt and controlled by mortals as magic. One story says that, while the idea was thought up by Lorkhan, it was Magnus who created the schematics and diagrams needed to construct the mortal plane. He is sometimes represented by an astrolabe, a telescope, or, more commonly, a staff. Cyrodilic legends say he can inhabit the bodies of powerful magicians and lend them his power. Associated with Zurin Arctus, the Underking.

Malacath (God of Curses): Malacath is the reanimated dung that was Trinimac. A somewhat weak but vengeful Daedra, the Dark Elves say he is also Malak, the god-king of the orcs. He always tests the Dunmer for physical weakness.

Malooc (Horde King): An enemy god of the Ra Gada. Led the goblins against the Redguards during the first era. Fled east when the army of the HoonDing overtook his goblin hordes.

Mauloch (Malacath): An Orcish god, Mauloch troubled the heirs of King Harald for a long time. Fled east after his defeat at the Battle of Dragon Wall, ca. 1E660. His rage was said to fill the sky with his sulphurous hatred, later called the "Year of Winter in Summer".

Mara (Goddess of Love): Nearly universal goddess. Origins started in mythic times as a fertility goddess. In Skyrim, Mara is a handmaiden of Kyne. In the Empire, she is Mother-Goddess. She is sometimes associated with Nir of the 'Anuad', the female principle of the cosmos that gave birth to creation. Depending on the religion, she is either married to Akatosh or Lorkhan, or the concubine of both.

Mehrunes Dagon (God of Destruction): Popular Daedric power. He is associated with natural dangers like fire, earthquakes, and floods. In some cultures, though, Dagon is merely a god of bloodshed and betrayal. He is an especially important deity in Morrowind, where he represents its near-inhospitable terrain.

Mephala (Androgyne): Mephala is the Webspinner, or the Spider God. In Morrowind, he/she was the ancestor that taught the Chimer the skills they would need to evade their enemies or to kill them with secret murder. Enemies were numerous in those days since the Chimer were a small faction. He/she, along with Boethiah, organized the clan systems that eventually became the basis for the Great Houses. He/she founded the Morag Tong. Also called the Anticipation of Vivec.

Molag Bal (God of Schemes, King of Rape): Daedric power of much importance in Morrowind. There, he is always the archenemy of Boethiah, the Prince of Plots. He is the main source of the obstacles to the Dunmer (and preceding Chimer) people. In the legends, Molag Bal always tries to upset the bloodlines of Houses or otherwise ruin Dunmeri 'purity'. A race of supermonsters, said to live in Molag Amur, are the result of his seduction of Vivec during the previous era.

Morihaus (First Breath of Man): Ancient cultural hero god of the Cyro-Nordics. Legend portrays him as the Taker of the Citadel, an act of mythic times that established Human control over the Valley Heartland. He is often associated with the Nordic powers of thu'um, and therefore with Kynareth.

Morwha (Teat God): Yokudan fertility goddess. Fundamental deity in the Yokudan pantheon, and the favorite of Tall Papa's wives. Still worshipped in various areas of Hammerfell, including Stros M'kai. Morwha is always portrayed as four-armed, so that she can 'grab more husbands'.

Nerevar (Godkiller): The Chimeri king of Resdayn, the Golden Age of old Veloth. Slain during the Battle of Red Mountain, Nerevar was the Herald of the Triune Way, and is the foremost of the saints of Dunmeri faith. He is said to have killed Dumac, the Last Dwarven King, and feasted on his heart.

Onsi (Boneshaver): Notable warrior god of the Yokudan Ra Gada, Onsi taught

Mankind how to pull their knives into swords.

Orkey (Old Knocker): A loan-god of the Nords, who seem to have taken up his worship during Aldmeri rule of Atmora. Nords believe they once lived as long as Elves until Orkey appeared; through heathen trickery, he fooled them into a bargain that 'bound them to the count of winters'. At one time, legends say, Nords only had a lifespan of six years due to Orkey's foul magic. Shor showed up, though, and, through unknown means, removed the curse, throwing most of it onto the nearby Orcs.

Phynaster: Hero-god of the Summerset Isles, who taught the Altmer how to naturally live another hundred years by using a shorter walking stride.

Rajhin (Footpad): Thief god of the Khajiiti, who grew up in the Black Kiergo section of Senchal. The most famous burglar in Elsweyr's history, Rajhin is said to have stolen a tattoo from the neck of Empress Kintyra as she slept.

Reman (The Cyrodiil): Culture god-hero of the Second Empire, Reman was the greatest hero of the Akaviri Trouble. Indeed, he convinced the invaders to help him build his own empire, and conquered all of Tamriel except for Morrowind. He instituted the rites of becoming Emperor, which included the ritual geas to the Amulet of Kings, a soulgem of immense power. His Dynasty was ended by the Dunmeri Morag Tong at the end of the first era. Also called the Worldly God.

Riddle'Thar (Two-Moons Dance): The cosmic order deity of the Khajiiti, the Riddle'Thar was revealed to Elsweyr by the prophet Rid-Thar-ri'Datta, the Mane. The Riddle'Thar is more a set of guidelines by which to live than a single entity, but some of his avatars like to appear as humble messengers of the gods. Also known as the Sugar God.

Ruptga (Tall Papa): Chief deity of the Yokudan pantheon. Ruptga, more commonly 'Tall Papa', was the first god to figure out how to survive the Hunger of Satakal. Following his lead, the other gods learned the 'Walkabout', or a process by which they can persist beyond one lifetime. Tall Papa set the stars in the sky to show lesser spirits how to do this, too. When there were too many spirits to keep track of, though, Ruptga created a helper out the dead skin of past worlds. This helper is Sep (see below), who later creates the world of mortals.

Satakal (The Worldskin): Yokudan god of everything. A fusion of the concepts of Anu and Padomay. Basically, Satakal is much like the Nordic Alduin, who destroys one world to begin the next. In Yokudan mythology, Satakal had done (and still does) this many times over, a cycle which prompted the birth of spirits that could survive the transition. These spirits ultimately become the Yokudan pantheon. Popular god of the Alik'r nomads.

Sheogorath (The Mad God): The fearful obeisance of Sheogorath is widespread, and is found in most Tamrielic quarters. Contemporary sources indicate that his roots are in Aldmeri creation stories; therein, he is 'born' when Lorkhan's divine spark is removed. One crucial myth calls him the 'Sithis-shaped hole' of the world.

Sheor (Bad Man): In Bretony, the Bad Man is the source of all strife. He seems to have started as the god of crop failure, but most modern theologians agree that he is a demonized version of the Nordic Shor, born during the dark years after the fall of Saarthal.

Sep (The Snake): Yokudan version of Lorkhan. Sep is born when Tall Papa creates someone to help him regulate the spirit trade. Sep, though, is driven crazy by the hunger of Satakal, and he convinces some of the gods to help him make an easier alternative to the Walkabout. This, of course, is the world as we know it, and the spirits who followed Sep become trapped here, to live out their lives as mortals. Sep is punished by Tall Papa for his transgressions, but his hunger lives on as a void in the stars, a 'non-space' that tries to upset mortal entry into the Far Shores.

Shezarr (God of Man): Cyrodilic version of Lorkhan, whose importance suffers when Akatosh comes to the fore of Imperial (really, Alessian) religion. Shezarr was the spirit behind all human undertaking, especially against Aldmeri aggression. He is sometimes associated with the founding of the first Cyrodilic battlemages. In the present age of racial tolerance, Shezarr is all but forgotten.

Shor (God of the Underworld): Nordic version of Lorkhan, who takes sides with Men after the creation of the world. Foreign gods (i.e., Elven ones) conspire against him and bring about his defeat, dooming him to the underworld. Atmoran myths depict him as a bloodthirsty warrior king who leads the Nords to victory over their Aldmeri oppressors time and again. Before his doom, Shor was the chief of the gods. Sometimes also called Children's God (see Orkey, above).

Sotha Sil (Mystery of Morrowind): God of the Dunmer, Sotha Sil is the least known of the divine Tribunal. He is said to be reshaping the world from his hidden, clockwork city.

Stendarr (God of Mercy): God of the Nine Divines, Stendarr has evolved from his Nordic origins into a deity of compassion or, sometimes, righteous rule. He is said to have accompanied Tiber Septim in his later years. In early Altmeri legends, Stendarr is the apologist of Men.

Stuhn (God of Ransom): Nordic precursor to Stendarr, brother of Tsun. Shield-thane of Shor, Stuhn was a warrior god that fought against the Aldmeri pantheon. He showed Men how to take, and the benefits of taking, prisoners of war.

Syrabane (Warlock's God): An Aldmeri god-ancestor of magic, Syrabane aided Bendu Olo in the Fall of the Sload. Through judicious use of his magical ring, Syrabane saved many from the scourge of the Thrassian Plague. He is also called the Apprentices' God, for he is a favorite of the younger members of the Mages Guild.

Tava (Bird God): Yokudan spirit of the air. Tava is most famous for leading the Yokudans to the isle of Herne after the destruction of their homeland. She has since become assimilated into the mythology of Kynareth. She is still very popular in Hammerfell among sailors, and her shrines can be found in most port cities.

Tiber Septim (Talos, the Dragonborn): Heir to the Seat of Sundered Kings, Tiber Septim is the most important hero-god of Mankind. He conquered all of Tamriel and ushered in the Third Era (and the Third Empire). Also called Ysmir, 'Dragon of the North'.

Trinimac: Strong god of the early Aldmer, in some places more popular than Auri-El. He was a warrior spirit of the original Elven tribes that led armies against the Men. Boethiah is said to have assumed his shape (in some stories, he even eats Trinimac) so that he could convince a throng of Aldmer to listen to him, which led to their eventual Chimeri conversion. He vanishes from the mythic stage after this, to return as the dread Malacath (Altmeri propaganda portrays this as the dangers of Dunmeri influence).

Tsun: Extinct Nordic god of trials against adversity. Died defending Shor from foreign gods.

Tu'whacca (Tricky God): Yokudan god of souls. Tu'whacca, before the creation of the world, was the god of Nobody Really Cares. When Tall Papa undertook the creation of the Walkabout, Tu'whacca found a purpose; he became the caretaker of the Far Shores, and continues to help Redguards find their way into the afterlife. His cult is sometimes associated with Arkay in the more cosmopolitan regions of Hammerfell.

Vivec (Master of Morrowind): Warrior-poet god of the Dunmer. Vivec is the invisible keeper of the holy land, ever vigilant against the dark gods of the Volcano. He/she has saved the Dunmeri people from certain death on numerous occasions, most notably when he/she taught them how to breathe water for a day so that he/she could flood Morrowind and kill the Akaviri invaders, ca. 2E572.

Xarxes: Xarxes is the god of ancestry and secret knowledge. He began as a scribe to Auri-El, and has kept track of all Aldmeri accomplishments, large and small, since the beginning of time. He created his wife, Oghma, from his favorite moments in history.

Yffre (God of the Forest): Most important deity of the Bosmeri pantheon. While Auri-El Time Dragon might be the king of the gods, the Bosmer revere Yffre as the spirit of 'the now'. According to the Wood Elves, after the creation of the mortal plane everything was in chaos. The first mortals were turning into plants and animals and back again. Then Yffre transformed himself into the first of the Ehlnofey, or 'Earth Bones'. After these laws of nature were established, mortals had a semblance of safety in the new world, because they could finally understand it. Yffre is sometimes called the Storyteller, for the lessons he taught the first Bosmer. Some Bosmer still possess the knowledge of the chaos times, which they can use to great effect (the Wild Hunt).

Ysmir (Dragon of the North): The Nordic aspect of Talos. He withstood the power of the Greybeards' voices long enough to hear their prophecy. Later, many Nords could not look on him without seeing a dragon.

Z'en (God of Toil): Bosmeri god of payment in kind. Studies indicate origins in both Argonian and Akaviri mythologies, perhaps introduced into Valenwood by Kothringi sailors. Ostensibly an agriculture deity, Z'en sometimes proves to be an entity of a much higher cosmic order. His worship died out shortly after the Knahaten Flu.

Zeht (God of Farms): Yokudan god of agriculture. Renounced his father after the world was created, which is why Tall Papa makes it so hard to grow food.

Zenithar (God of Work and Commerce, Trader God): Member of the Nine Divines,

Zenithar is understandably associated with Z'en. In the Empire, however, he is a far more cultivated god of merchants and middle nobility. His worshippers say, despite his mysterious origins, Zenithar is the god 'that will always win'.

Lives of the Saints

If you would be wise, model your lives on the lives of the saints.

If you would learn valor, follow St. Nerevar the Captain, patron of Warriors and Statesmen. Lord Nerevar helped to unite the barbarian Dunmer tribes into a great nation, culminating in his martyrdom when leading the Dunmer to victory against the evil Dwemer and the traitorous House Dagoth in the Battle of Red Mountain.

If you would learn daring, follow Saint Veloth the Pilgrim, Patron of Outcasts and Spiritual Seekers. Saint Veloth, prophet and mystic, led the Dunmer out of the decadent home country of the Summerset Isles and into the promised land of Morrowind. Saint Veloth also taught the difference between the Good and Bad Daedra, and won the aid of the Good Daedra for his people while teaching how to carefully negotiate with the Bad Daedra.

If you would learn generosity, follow Saint Rilms the Barefooted, Patron of Pilgrims and Beggars. Saint Rilms gave away her shoes, then dressed and appeared as a beggar to better acquaint herself with the poor.

If you would learn self-respect and respect for others, follow Saint Aralor the Penitent, Patron of Tanners and Miners. This foul criminal repented his sins and traveled a circuit of the great pilgrimages on his knees.

If you would learn mercy and its fruits, follow Saint Seryn the Merciful, Patron of Brewers, Bakers, Distillers. This pure virgin of modest aspect could heal all diseases at the price of taking the disease upon herself. Tough-minded and fearless, she took on the burdens of others, and bore those burdens to an honored old age.

If you would learn fierce justice, follow Saint Felms the Bold, Patron of Butchers and Fishmongers. This brave warlord slew the Nord invaders and drove them from our lands. He could neither read nor write, receiving inspiration directly from the lips of Almsivi.

If you would learn pride of race and tribe, follow Saint Roris the Martyr, Patron of Furnishers and Caravaners. Captured by Argonians just before the Arnesian War, Roris proudly refused to renounce the Tribunal faith, and withstood the cruel tortures of Argonian sorcerers. Vengeance and justice for the martyred Saint Roris was the rallying cry of the Arnesian War.

If you would learn the rule of law and justice, follow Saint Olms the Just, Patron of Chandlers and Clerks. Founder of the Ordinators, Saint Olms conceived and articulated the fundamental principles of testing, ordeal, and repentance.

If you would learn benevolence, follow Saint Delyn the Wise, Patron of Potters and Glassmakers. Saint Delyn was head of House Indoril, a skilled lawyer, and author of many learned treatises on Tribunal law and custom.

If you would learn the love of peace, follow Saint Meris the Peacemaker, Patron of Farmers and Laborers. As a little girl, Saint Meris showed healing gifts, and trained as a Healer. She ended a long and bloody House War, intervening on the battlefield in her white robe to heal warriors and spellcrafters without regard to faction. The troops of all House adopted white robes as her standard, and refused to shed the blood of their brethren.

If you would learn reverence, follow Saint Llothis the Pious, Patron of Tailors and Dyers. Contemporary and companion of the Tribunals, and the best-loved Alma Rula of the Tribunal Temple, he formulated the central rituals and principles of the New Temple Faith. Saint Llothis is the symbolic mortal bridge between the gods and the faithful, and the archetypal priest.

The Doors of the Spirit

The Ancestors are among us. They are never farther away than the Waiting Door.

The Ancestors are not departed. The dead are not under the earth. Their spirits are in the restless wind, in the fire's voice, in the foot-smoothed step. Pay heed to these things, and you will know your absent kin.

Pay reverence through gift and prayer. Acquaint the Ancestors with your affairs, with your comings and goings, with your blessings and trials.

From the Waiting Door comes your protection. Heed the spirits, who are the guardians of your hearth, teachers of wisdom, counselors of fortune, seers of fate.

Each bone is a door through the wall of the world. Each bone is the road, with Wisdom and Power the travelers. Each bone is the ghost fence that guards us from evil.

Honor the Ancestors upon your hearths, within your halls, in the community of your temples, in the solitude of your tombs.

Guard your Ancestors from beasts, from thieves, from profane priest and sorcerers. Let no creature steal your spirits, for the plundered hearth is diminished, and the plundered tomb is shamed.

Live in One World with your spirits. Honor the spirits within and without you. Do not grieve for the dead. Take shelter in their arms, and pay heed to their words.

Spirit of Nirn

Lorkhan is the Spirit of Nirn, the god of all mortals. This does not mean all mortals necessarily like him or even know him. Most elves hate him, thinking creation as that act which sundered them from the spirit realm. Most Humans revere him, or aspects of him, as the herald of existence. The creation of the Mortal Plane, the Mundus, Nirn, is a source of mental anguish to all living things; all souls know deep down they came originally from somewhere else, and that Nirn is a cruel and crucial step to what comes next. What is this next? Some wish to return to the original state, the spirit realm, and that Lorkhan is the Demon that hinders their way; to them Nirn is a prison, an illusion to escape. Others think that Lorkhan created the world as the testing ground for transcendence; to them the spirit realm was already a prison, that true escape is now finally possible.

The Talos Mistake

by Leonora Venatus Imperial Liaison to the Aldmeri Dominion

As citizens of the Empire, all are of course familiar with the deeds of Emperor Tiber Septim. But it is the Emperor's ascent to godhood, as Talos, that is the subject of this work.

Until Tiber Septim's death, there had been but Eight Divines: Akatosh, Dibella, Arkay, Zenithar, Stendarr, Mara, Kynareth, and Julianos. These gods were, and are, worshipped throughout the Empire. And while some may have different names in the varying provinces (for example, Akatosh is known as "Auri-El" to the Aldmer; and Arkay is sometimes known as "Ar'Kay"), all are recognized and revered by all races and cultures of Tamriel.

But when Tiber Septim passed to Aetherius, there came to be a Ninth Divine — Talos, also called Ysmir, the "Dragon of the North." The man who was so loved in life became worshipped in death. Indeed, it can be argued that Talos, the Ninth Divine, became even more important than the Eight that had preceded him, at least to humans. For he was a god who was once just a man, and through great deeds actually managed to ascend to godhood. And if one human could achieve such a feat — couldn't it be done again? Couldn't all humans aspire to achieve divinity?

So we thought, we humans. And so we continued to worship Talos, and revere him as the ultimate hero-god. But that was then. This is now. And now, we know the truth:

We were wrong.

As citizens of the Empire, we all experienced the horrors of the Great War. And it was not until the signing of the White-Gold Concordat, the treaty between the Empire and the Aldmeri Dominion, that we once again knew peace. One of the most important stipulations of that treaty, as every Imperial citizen is well aware, is that Talos can no longer be worshipped as a god. This edict shook the very foundations of the Empire. There were those who rebelled against the law. Indeed, some still do.

But the citizens of the Empire must know this: the Emperor did not agree to outlaw the worship of Talos because it was demanded by the Thalmor, the ruling body of the Aldmeri Dominion.

The Emperor agreed to the outlaw of the worship of Talos because it was the right thing to do.

Today, the Emperor, and indeed the Empire itself, recognizes that allowing the worship of Talos was a mistake. For by doing so, by allowing the worship of Talos as a Divine, the Empire actually did its people a great disservice: for this only succeeded in weakening the memory of the man Tiber Septim and his many extraordinary (though mortal) deeds; and pushing people away from the Eight Divines, the true gods, who do deserve our love and reverence.

And so, the Empire admits it was wrong. The Talos Mistake will not be repeated.

May we find centuries of peace and prosperity with our new Thalmor friends, and continue to share a spirituality that binds together all the cultures and races of Tamriel.

Pension of the Ancestor Moth

To be read by all novitiates of the Temple:

The Order of the Ancestor Moth is as ancient as it is noble. We nurture and celebrate our beloved ancestors, whose spirits are manifest in the Ancestor Moths. Each moth carries the fjyron of an ancestor's spirit. Loosely translated as the "will to peace," the fjyron can be sung into the silk produced by the Ancestor Moths. When the silk is in turn spun into cloth and embroidered with the genealogy of the correct Ancestor, clothing of wondrous power can be made.

Adepts of our order are gifted with prescient powers. The wisdom of the ancestors can sing the future into the present. For this reason, our order and our order alone has been given the privilege to interpret the Elder Scrolls. These writings exceed even the gods, both aedra and daedra. Such insight into the inner fabric of reality comes at a price. Each reading of the Elder Scrolls is more profound than the last. Each leaves the priest blind for longer, and longer periods of time. Finally, the last reading achieves a nearly sublime understanding of that scroll's contents, but the priest is left permanently blinded to the light of this world. No longer can he read the scrolls.

This Monastery is dedicated to the service of these noble members of our order. They now live out their lives with the Ancestor Moths that they so love. Their underground demesnes are well suited to the moths. They raise and nurture the fragile creatures, singing to them constantly. They harvest the silk and spin it into bolts of cloth. They weave the cloth, embroidering it with the genealogies and histories of the ancestors that spun the silk. This is their new life.

As they tend the Ancestor Moths, so we tend the blind monks. While they toil in dark, we serve in the light. They need food and water. We provide. They need tools and furniture. We provide. They need secrecy and anonymity. We provide. They need purveyors to sell the fruit of their labors. We provide.

At one time, we also provided protection. Many generations ago, Gudrun came to our temple. Newly blinded by visions of what was to be, she brought with her new teachings. The visions of the ancestors foresaw the need of the monks to defend themselves. They train and practice the teachings of Gudrun constantly. They are masters of the sword of no sword, the axes of no axe.

As a novitiate, you will learn the teachings of Gudrun. You will learn the way of the peaceful fist. You will learn to serve the blind monks. You will learn to provide. In time, you may attain the peace and insight of the Ancestor Moths.

The Reclamations:
The Fall of the Tribunal and the
Rise of the New Temple

by Thara of Rihad

The destruction of Vivec City and the subsequent eruption of Red Mountain in 4E 5 was not just a crisis in terms of the physical destruction it caused — it also cut deeply into the ancient religious beliefs of the Dunmer. The fall of the Ministry of Truth was the last straw in the tottering support for the Temple's worship of Almalexia, Sotha Sil, and Vivec. With all three of the Tribunes now widely believed dead or disappeared, what had been a simmering schism within the ranks of the Temple priesthood burst into the open.

While outsiders may never know the full tale of this internal struggle, when the smoke cleared a few years later, the former Dissident Priests were in full control of the Temple heirarchy, with Tribunal loyalists either purged or recanted. The so-called "New Temple" now declared the worship of the Tribunes a result of misguided teaching, blaming the mistakes on the former Tribunal. The Temple now taught that the daedra venerated by the Ashlander tribes (Azura, Mephala and Boethia) were the "true way" and should be revered by the Dunmer people. Fittingly, the daedra were named the "Reclamations," as if they were reclaiming their status from the Tribunal.

In an elegant comprise, no doubt intended to reconcile the large majority of the Temple priesthood who were neither Dissidents nor fanatic Tribunal loyalists, Almalexia, Sotha Sil and Vivec were relegated to the status of "saints," a traditional way to venerate the most honored Dunmer ancestors. This apparently satisfied enough of the existing priesthood that the New Temple was able to maintain at least a semblance of outward continuity.

The rise of the New Temple almost completely vindicated the previously persecuted Ashlanders, who had continued to worship the three daedra throughout the Tribunal's rule. The Ashlanders are now lauded as the keepers of the old ways and having "true vision." It is now quite common for many of the Dunmer people to make the arduous pilgrimages into the ash wastes to seek the counsel of the Wise Women. These women have supposedly opened the eyes of those who they claim were "blinded by the Tribunal," and directly connect the eruption of the Red Mountain and the Argonian invasion to the anger of the three daedra.

House Indoril, whose fortunes were so entwined with the Tribunal Temple, suffered greatly from its fall. While House Indoril still technically exists, the priesthood of the Temple are now considered one and the same with House Indoril — those who become priests are now considered to have "joined Indoril." The political power of the Indoril has thus passed entirely into the hands of the Temple (although members of the old House Indoril are still over-represented in the priesthood).

The rise of the New Temple has a number of interesting parallels with the rise of House Redoran — each filled the vacuum of power resulting from the crisis of Red Year. How durable these new arrangements will prove, religious and political, remains to be seen. The span of two centuries is quite brief in the long history of the ancient Dunmer people.

Nchunak's Fire and Faith

This book is a translated account of Nchunak's travels among the various colonies of the Dwemer explaining the theories of Kagrenac. I made inquiry as to the state of enlightenment among the people he spoke for. He answered that with respect to the theories of Kagrenac, there was but one scholar near who could guide the people through the maze that leads to true misunderstanding.

He informed me, however, that in Kherakah the precepts of Kagrenac were taught. He said that nothing pleased him more than to see the Dwemer of Kherakah, the most learned people in the world, studying Kagrenac's words and giving consideration to their place in the life to come, and where neither planar division nor the numeration of amnesia nor any other thing of utility was more valued than the understanding of the self and its relationship to the Heart.

I was gracious enough to receive this as a high compliment, and, removing my helm, I thanked him and departed with an infinity of bows.

A Dream of Sovngarde

In a few hours, I will likely be dead.

My men and I, Nords of Skyrim all, will soon join with the Emperor's legions to attack the Imperial City. The Aldmeri are entrenched within and our losses will be severe. It is a desperate gambit, for if we do not reclaim the city, we will lose the war.

Last night I prayed to mighty Talos for courage and strength in the battle to come. In these last cold hours before the sun rises, I sit down to write this account of a dream I had not long after.

I believe this dream was the answer to my prayers, and I would pass along the wisdom it contained to my kinsmen, for the battles they will fight in the years after my passing.

In the dream, I walked through mists toward the sound of laughter, merriment and the songs of the north. The mists soon cleared, and before me lay a great chasm. Waters thundered over its brim, and so deep it was, I could not see the bottom.

A great bridge made all of whale-bone was the only means to cross, and so I took it. It was only a few steps onto the bridge that I encountered a warrior, grim and strong. "I am Tsun, master of trials," he said to me, his voice booming and echoing upon the walls of the high mountains all around us.

With a wave, he bade me pass on. I knew in my heart that I was granted passage only because I was a visitor. Should the hour come when I return here after my mortal life, the legends say that I must best this dread warrior in single combat.

Beyond the bridge, a great stone longhouse rose up before me, so tall as to nearly touch the clouds. Though it took all my strength, I pushed open the towering oaken door and beheld the torch-lit feast hall.

Here were assembled the greatest heroes of the Nords, all drinking mead poured from great kegs and singing battle-songs. Suckling pigs turned on a long iron spit over a roaring fire. My mouth watered at the smell of roast meat, and my heart was glad to hear the songs of old.

"Come forth!" cried out a hoary man who sat upon a high wooden chair. This I knew to be Ysgramor, father of Skyrim and the Nords. I approached and knelt before him.

"You find yourself in Sovngarde, hall of the honored dead. Now, what would you have of me, son of the north?" he bellowed.

"I seek counsel," said I, "for tomorrow we fight a desperate battle and my heart is full of fear."

Ysgramor raised his tankard to his lips and drank until the cup was empty. Then he spoke once more.

"Remember this always, son of the north — a Nord is judged not by the manner in which he lived, but the manner in which he died."

With that, he cast aside his flagon, raised his fist in the air and roared a great cheer. The other heroes rose to their feet and cheered in answer.

The sound still rang in my ears when I awoke. I gathered my men and told them of my vision. The words seemed to fill their hearts with courage.

The horns are blowing, and the banners are raised. The time has come to muster. May Talos grant us victory this day, and if I am found worthy, may I once again look upon that great feast hall.

- Skardan Free-Winter

Sovngarde: A Reexamination

by Bereditte Jastal

Speculation regarding Sovngarde, the Nordic Hall of Valor

Death. It is something we all face. Or do we?

Just ask the nearest Nord what he thinks of the end of life, and you'll likely be treated to a horrific story of blood, bone and viscera, of courageous deeds and heartbreaking sorrow. Carnage notwithstanding, there may be even more to death than the average Nord warrior realizes. New evidence suggests a life beyond the battlefield, where a valiant Nord may live forever, downing mead and engaging in contests of strength and skill. But in order to fully understand the possibility of a Nord's eternal life after death, one must first reexamine the legends surrounding that most wondrous of warrior's retreats — Sovngarde.

According to the ancient writings and oral traditions of the Nords, going back as far as the Late Merethic Era, there exists a place so magnificent, so honored, that the entrance lies hidden from view. Sovngarde, it is called, built by the god Shor to honor those Nords who have proven their mettle in war. Within this "Hall of Valor" time as we know it has no meaning. The concepts of life and death are left on the doorstep, and those within exist in a sort of self-contained euphoria, free of pain, suffering and the worst malady a Nord could suffer — boredom.

But just how well hidden the entrance to Sovngarde is has been a matter of much scholarly debate, and there are those who believe Shor's great hall is just a myth, for there are no actual accounts from Nords who have experienced the wonders of Sovngarde then returned to tell the tale. Not that this has stopped anyone from looking. Some Nords spend a lifetime searching for the mysterious hidden entrance to Sovngarde. Most return home sad and broken, their hearts heavy with failure. They'll never know the pleasure of a mead flagon that never empties, or a wrestling tournament without end.

What, some may ask, does the entrance to Sovngarde have to do with death? Everything, according to a series of ancient parchments recently discovered in the attic of a deceased Nord's home in Cyrodiil. What at first seemed to be a series of love letters was later found to be a correspondence between one Felga Four-Fingers, a medium of some note, and the ghost of a Nord warrior named Rolf the Large.

According to the parchments, Rolf had spent his entire life searching for the entrance to Sovngarde, without success. He was returning home to his village of Skyrim when

he was waylaid by a band of giants. Rolf fought bravely, but was quickly killed, and the giants proceeded to play catch with his head. Amazingly, all of this was seen by Rolf in ghostly form as he drifted away from the scene, soaring upwards into the heavens, where he finally arrived... in the magnificent hall of Sovngarde!

Rolf could not believe his good fortune, and his foolishness for not having realized the truth so many years before. For death was the entrance to Sovngarde. So he was told by Shor himself, who greeted Rolf the Large as a brother, and personally handed him a leg of roast mutton and the hand of a comely wench. Sovngarde, Shor told him, can be entered by any Nord who dies valiantly in honorable combat.

It is time for Nords to learn the truth. Eternal life can be theirs, without the need to spend an entire mortal life in vain pursuit of something completely unattainable. In the end, all valiant Nords can enter Sovngarde. Dismemberment, decapitation or evisceration seems a small price to pay for the chance to spend an eternity in Shor's wondrous hall.

The Amulet of Kings

by Wenengrus Monhona

In the first years of the First Era, a powerful race of Elves called the Ayleids, or the Heartland High Elves, ruled central Tamriel with an iron hand. The high and haughty Ayleids relied on their patrons, the treacherous Daedra Lords, to provide armies of daedra and dead spirits; with these fearless magical armies, the Ayleids preyed without mercy upon the young races of men, slaughtering or enslaving them at their whim.

On behalf of the suffering human races, St. Alessia, the first in the line of Cyrodiils, sought the aid of Akatosh, the Dragon God of Time, and ruler of the noble Aedra. Akatosh, looking with pity upon the plight of men, drew precious blood from his own

heart, and blessed St. Alessia with this blood of Dragons, and made a Covenant that so long as Alessia's generations were true to the dragon blood, Akatosh would endeavor to seal tight the Gates of Oblivion, and to deny the armies of daedra and undead to their enemies, the Daedra-loving Ayleids.

In token of this Covenant, Akatosh gave to Alessia and her descendants the Amulet of Kings and the Eternal Dragonfires of the Imperial City. Thus does Alessia become the first gem in the Cyrodilic Amulet of Kings. The gem is the Red Diamond in the middle of the Amulet. This is the Symbol of the Empire and later taken as the symbol of the Septim line. It is surrounded by eight other gems, one for each of the divines.

So long as the Empire shall maintain its worship of Akatosh and his kin, and so long as Alessia's heirs shall bear the Amulet of Kings, Akatosh and his divine kin maintain a strong barrier between Tamriel and Oblivion, so that mortal man need never again fear the devastating summoned hosts of the Daedra Lords.

But if the Empire should slacken in its dedication to the Nine Divines, or if the blood of Alessia's heirs should fail, then shall the barriers between Tamriel and the Daedric realms fall, and Daedra-worshippers might summon lesser Daedra and undead spirits to trouble the races of men.

The Last King of the Ayleids

by Herminia Cinna

The Ayleids, or Heartland High Elves, ruled Cyrodiil in the long ages of Myth before the beginning of recorded history. One of the earliest recorded dates, in fact, is the Fall of White Gold Tower in 1E 243, which is commonly assumed to mark the end of the Ayleids.

Although Ayleid rule over all of Cyrodiil was indeed broken in 1E 243, this was only one of the most obvious stages near the end of a long decline. The first two centuries of the First Era saw increasing strife between the great Ayleid lords of Cyrodiil. Alessia appears to have taken advantage of a period of civil war to launch her uprising. Imperial historians have traditionally attributed her victory to intervention from Skyrim, but it appears that she had at least as much help from rebel Ayleid lords during the siege of White Gold Tower.

The popular image of the Ayleids as brutal slavemasters is based in fact, of course, but it is less well-known that a number of Ayleid princes continued to rule parts of Cyrodiil after 263, as vassals of the new Empress of Cyrodiil. This suggests either that Ayleid rule was not universally detested, or that Alessia and her successors were more pragmatic than is traditionally believed, or perhaps some of both.

In any event, excavations at a number of Ayleid sites show continued occupation and even expansion during the so-called Late Ayleid Period (1E 243 – c. 498). At first, many Ayleid lords continued to rule as vassals of the new human regime. In some cases, Ayleid supporters of Alessia were even rewarded with new lands taken from slain enemies. It is not clear to what extent human slavery continued under the Cyrodilic Empire. Humans continued to dwell in the Ayleid-ruled areas of Cyrodiil, but there is nothing definitive to show under what terms.

This was an uneasy relationship from the beginning, and was not destined to last long. Resentment at the continued presence of Ayleid nobles within the Empire was a contributing factor to the rise of the so-called Alessian Order founded by Maruhk. The first victims of the Alessians were the Ayleids of Cyrodiil. In the early 300s, the surviving Ayleid communities in human-ruled areas were obliterated one by one, the refugees temporarily swelling the power of the remaining Ayleid lordships.

Then in 361, the Alessians gained control of the Empire and enforced the Alessian Doctrines throughout its domain. The Ayleid lordships were abolished. Enforcement of this decree does not appear to have required much direct violence — it seems that by this point the balance of power was so overwhelmingly against them, and their fate so long foreshadowed, that most of the remaining Ayleids simply left Cyrodiil, eventually being absorbed into the Elven populations of Valenwood and High Rock. Indeed, the rise of the Direnni Hegemony may be linked to this exodus of Ayleids from Cyrodiil (a connection so far little studied by historians).

Still, a remnant Ayleid population seems to have survived the rule of the Alessians, because we hear of "the last king of the Ayleids" joining the battle of Glenumbria Moors where the Dirennis decisively defeated the Alessians in 482. How this king's people survived the preceding century is unknown. We do not even know who they were, although recent research points to Nenalata as the possible resting place of this "last king." Unfortunately, in the current state of the Empire, funds are no longer available for proper scientific investigation of such extensive ruins, so the answer to these questions will have to be left to future generations.

Magic from the Sky

by Irlav Jarol

The ancient Ayleids believed that Nirn was composed of four basic elements — earth, water, air, and light — and of these four elements, they believed the most sublime form of light was star light. The stars are our links to the plane of Aetherius, the source of all magical power, and therefore, light from the stars is the most potent and exalted of all magical powers.

From time to time, fragments of Aetherius fall from the heavens. The people know these fragments as 'shooting stars', and from time to time, such Aetherial fragments are found on Nirn. The most common varieties are known as 'meteoric iron'; this metal is prized by armorers and enchanters for its properties in the forging of enchanted weapons and armors. This meteoric iron is also the primary component in 'Ayleid Wells,' ancient enchanted artifacts found throughout Cyrodiil.

Another, rarer form of Aetherial fragment is called 'meteoric glass'. It is from such fragments that other rare Ayleid enchanted artifacts are crafted — Welkynd Stones and Varla Stones.

Ayleids Wells are scattered across Cyrodiil's landscape. Their siting is a mystery; they are not associated with any known Ayleid cities or settlements. It is presumed that, in some manner, they harvest magical power from starlight. It is also suggested, without evidence or support, that they are located at the meeting points of ancient lines of magical power; however, modern arcane arts have discovered no perceptible evidence of such lines of power.

Those with magical talents can draw magicka from Ayleid wells to restore their own reservoirs of magical power. No ritual or arcane knowledge is necessary, suggesting that these wells were designed to serve persons not skilled in the magical arts. Once drained, the wells replenish again only at magical midnight. Once recharged, they appear to radiate magical power back into the sky, which prompts some to theorize they are also objects with religious or magical ritual significance — perhaps a means of offering magic back to the heavens.

Welkynd Stones [Aldmeris — "sky stone," "heaven stone"; literally, "sky child"] are pieces of cut and enchanted meteoric glass which apparently act as storage devices for magical power. A magical talent can restore his reseroirs of magicka from such stones. Alas, the means of restoring power to these stones may have been lost with the Ayleids. Currently, these objects simply crumble to dust after they have been used.

Great Welkynd Stones are exceptionally large pieces of enchanted meteoric glass. Scholars believe that at the heart of each ancient Ayleid city, a Great Welkynd Stone was the source of the settlement's magical enchantments. It may be that these great stones were linked to the lesser stones, restoring and maintaining their power. In any case, research on these Great Welkynd Stones is impossible, since all the known Ayleid ruins have been looted of their great stones, and no examples of these great stones are known to survive.

Another rare enchanted item found in Ayleid ruins is called a Varla Stone [Aldmeris — "star stone"]. Varla Stones are remarkably powerful, enabling untrained users to restore magical energy to any number of enchanted items. Because of their great value and utility, these items are also extremely rare, but since they are small and easily concealed, diligent explorers may still occasionally come across them in any Ayelid ruin.

Ayleid Wells. Welkynd Stones. Varla Stones. Consider, then, these marvels of magical enchantment. Are we then to conclude that the Ayleids were a superior race and culture? Did they so exceed us in art and craft that they mock the feeble powers of Third Era Wizards?

Never! The Ayleids were powerful, yes, and cunning, but they were neither good nor wise, and so they were struck down. Their works have passed from Nirn, save these rare and sparkling treasures. Their ancient cities are dark and empty, save for the grim revenants and restless spirits condemned forever to walk the halls, keeping their melancholy vigils over bones and dust.

Treatise on Ayleidic Cities: Varsa Baalim and the Nefarivigum Test of Dagon

Chapter the Tenth

I will not be the first scholar to point to a combination of benign intent and arrogance on behalf of the Ayleids as the source of many ruinous affairs for the old heartland elves.

The Nefarivigum, a foul construct of Mehrunes Dagon, was erected to be ever watchful for the pilgrim who would approach it and best an unknown trial of worth. It is said that such a pilgrim would be rewarded with the blessing of Mehrunes Razor, a vicious blade through which Dagon himself can claim the very souls of those it strikes.

Benign intent compelled Ayleid folk to seek out the Nefarivigum. Arrogance let them believe themselves capable of disbarring any who would seek the Razor. So was built Varsa Baalim, a great, ringed, labyrinthine city, during the height of Ayleid rule.

Sure as death, pilgrims came to Varsa Baalim, and for years the Elves drove back many, until it came to pass that a vampire slipped into the city unnoticed. Merfolk were touched with the foul affliction, throwing the city into a gathering storm of madness and ruin, and soon it seemed none was left to prevent the Razor from being recovered.

Then, suddenly, Varsa Baalim was gone. Historic accounts dispute whether it happened through some final safety, a natural cataclysm, or by the touch of the Divines themselves. Whatever the cause, history agrees on the result: the mountains of the Eastern Niben swallowed Varsa Baalim, and the Nefarivigum with it, where has remained hidden since the early days of the First Era.

If the tale is true, then somewhere on the eastern fringes of the Niben Valley, where man's rule has scarcely reached through the years, the Nefarivigum still lies in wait, among a city of unliving abominations entombed within the cold bowels of the mountain.

The Adabal-a

Editor's Note: The Adabal-a is traditionally believed to be the memoirs of Morihaus, consort to Alessia the Slave Queen. While this cannot be historically verified, the Adabal-a is certainly among the oldest written accounts to come down to us from the early First Era.

PELINAL'S DEATH

And in the blood-floored throne room of White-Gold, the severed head of Pelinal spoke to the winged-bull, Morihaus, demigod lover of Al-Esh, saying, "Our enemies have undone me, and spread my body into hiding. In mockery of divine purpose, the Ayleids cut me into eighths, for they are obsessed with this number."

And Morihaus, confused, snorted through his ring, saying, "Your crusades went beyond her counsel, Whitestrake, but I am a bull, and therefore reckless in my wit. I think I would go and gore our prisoners if you had left any alive. You are blood-made-glorious, uncle, and will come again, as fox animal or light. Cyrod is still ours."

Then Pelinal spoke again for the last time: "Beware, Morihaus, beware! With the foresight of death I know now that my foe yet lives, bitter knowledge to take to my grave. Better that I had died believing myself the victor. Although cast beyond the doors of night, he will return. Be vigilant! I can no longer shield the host of Men from Umaril's retribution."

ALESSIA'S YOUTH DURING THE SLAVE-YEARS

Perrif's original tribe is unknown, but she grew up in Sard, anon Sardarvar Leed, where the Ayleids herded in men from across all the Niben: kothri, nede, al-gemha, men-of-'kreath (though these were later known to be imported from the North), keptu, men-of-ge (who were eventually destroyed when the Flower King Nilichi made great sacrifice to an insect god whose name is lost), al-hared, men-of-ket, others; but this was Cyrod, the heart of the imperatum saliache, where men knew no freedom, even to keep family, or choice of name except in secret, and so to their alien masters all of these designations were irrelevant.

Men were given over to the lifting of stones, and the draining of the fields, and the upkeep of temple and road; or to become art-tortures for strange pleasures, as in the wailing wheels of Vindasel and the gut-gardens of Sercen; and flesh-sculpture, which was everywhere among the slaves of the Ayleids in those days; or, worse, the realms of the Fire King Hadhuul, where the begetting of drugs drawn from the admixture of daedrons into living hosts let one inhale new visions of torment, and children were set aflame for nighttime tiger sport.

MORIHAUS EXPLAINS ALESSIA'S NAMES

Then Morihaus said to them: "In your tales you have many names for her: Al-Esh, given to her in awe, that when translated sounds like a redundancy, 'the high high', from which come the more familiar corruptions: Aleshut, Esha, Alessia. You knew her as Paravant, given to her when crowned, 'first of its kind', by which the gods meant a mortal worthy of the majesty that is killing-questing-healing, which is also Paraval, Pevesh, Perrethu, Perrif, and, in my case, for it is what I called her when we were lovers: Paravania."

"Though she is gone to me, she remains bathed in stars, first Empress, Lady of Heaven, Queen-ut-Cyrod."

And they considered themselves full-answered, and departed.

Trials of St. Alessia

katosh made a covenant with Alessia in those days so long ago. He gathered the tangled skeins of Oblivion, and knit them fast with the bloody sinews of his Heart, and gave them to Alessia, saying, 'This shall be my token to you, that so long as your blood and oath hold true, yet so shall my blood and oath be true to you. This token shall be the Amulet of Kings, and the Covenant shall be made between us, for I am the King of Spirits, and you are the Queen of Mortals. As you shall stand witness for all Mortal Flesh, so shall I stand witness for all Immortal Spirits.'

And Akatosh drew from his breast a burning handful of his Heart's blood, and he gave it into Alessia's hand, saying, 'This shall also be a token to you of our joined blood and pledged faith. So long as you and your descendants shall wear the Amulet of Kings, then shall this dragonfire burn — an eternal flame — as a sign to all men and gods of our faithfulness. So long as the dragonfires shall burn, to you, and to all generations, I swear that my Heart's blood shall hold fast the Gates of Oblivion.

So long as the Blood of the Dragon runs strong in her rulers, the glory of the Empire shall extend in unbroken years. But should the dragonfires fail, and should no heir of our joined blood wear the Amulet of Kings, then shall the Empire descend into darkness, and the Demon Lords of Misrule shall govern the land.'

— From the liturgy of the Re-Kindling of the Dragonfire

The Chronicles of the Holy Brothers of Marukh Volume IV

Or, The Cleansing of the Fane

Editor's Note: This is the only surviving fragment of the chronicle of this First Era sect of the Alessian Order. It seems to have been kept at their great monastic complex at Lake Canulus, which was razed during the War of Righteousness (1E 2321) and its archives destroyed or dispersed. Note also that Alessian scribes of this time customarily dated events from the Apotheosis of Alessia (1E 266).

ere is recorded the events of the Year 127 of the Blessed Alessia.

In this year was the day darkened over all lands, and the sun was all as it were Masser but three days old, and the stars about him at midday. This was on the fifth of First Seed. All who saw it were dismayed, and said that a great event should come hereafter. So it did, for that same year issued forth a great concourse of devils from the ancient Elvish temple Malada, such had not been seen since the days of King Belharza. These devils greatly afflicted the land such that no man could plow, or reap, or seed, and the people appealed to the brothers of Marukh for succour. And then Abbot Cosmas gathered all the brothers and led them to Malada, also known as the High Fane in the Elvish tongue, and came against it with holy fire, and the foul demons were destroyed, and many devilish relics and books found therein were burned. And the land had peace for many years.

Shezarr and the Divines

by Faustillus Junius, Subcurator of

Ancient Theology and Paleonumerology, Imperial Library

he position Shezarr enjoys in Cyrodilic worship if often misconstrued. He, and a thousand other deities, have sizeable cults in the Imperial City. Shezarr is especially venerated in the Colovian West, though he is called Shor there, as the West Kings are resolutely, and religiously, Nordic.

The haziness of Shezarr's relationship to the Divines (he is often called their 'Missing Sibling') begins with St. Alessia, the so-called 'Slave Queen of Cyrodiil,' the founder figure of the original Cyrodilic Empire. In the earliest Cyro-Nordic stories of the Heartland, Shezarr fought against the Ayleids (the 'Heartland Highelves') on mankind's behalf. Then, for some unknown reason, he vanishes from the stage (presumably to help other humans elsewhere), and, without his leadership, the Ayleids conquer the humans and enslave them.

This slavery lasts for generations. The isolated humans eventually begin to venerate the pantheon of their masters, or at least assimilate so much of High Elven religious practices into their native traditions that the two become indistinguishable.

In 1E242, under the leadership of Alessia, her demigod lover, Morihaus-Breath-of-

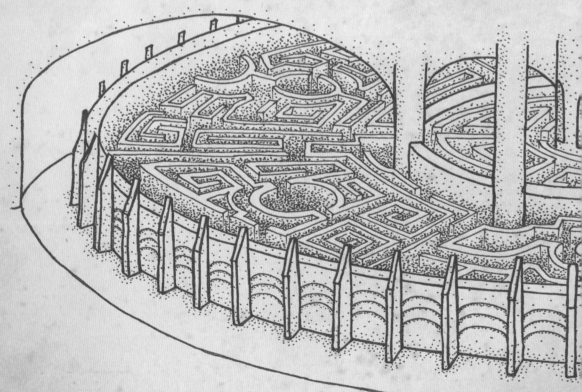

Kyne, and the infamous Pelinal Whitestrake, the Cyrodilic humans revolt. When Skyrim lends its armies to the Slave-Queen of the South, the revolution succeeds. The Ayleid Hegemonies are quickly overthrown. Shortly thereafter, White Gold Tower is captured by Alessia's forces, and she promptly declares herself the first Empress of Cyrodiil. Part of the package meant that she had to become the High Priestess of Akatosh, as well.

Akatosh was an Aldmeri god, and Alessia's subjects were as-yet unwilling to renounce their worship of the Elven pantheon. She found herself in a very sensitive political situation. She needed to keep the Nords as her allies, but they were (at that time) fiercely opposed to any adoration of Elven deities. On the other hand, she could not force her subjects to revert back to the Nordic pantheon, for fear of another revolution. Therefore, concessions were made and Empress Alessia instituted a new religion: the Eight Divines, an elegant, well-researched synthesis of both pantheons, Nordic and Aldmeri.

Shezarr, as a result, had to change. He could no longer be the bloodthirsty anti-Aldmer warlord of old. He could not disappear altogether either, or the Nords would have withdrawn their support of her rule. In the end, he had become "the spirit behind all human undertaking." Even though this was merely a thinly-disguised, watered-down version of Shor, it was good enough for the Nords.

As for why Tiber Septim has not attempted to 'revitalize' Shezarr during his wars against the Aldmeri Dominion, we can only speculate that, at this time, memories of the Alessian Order's follies (the Dragon Break, the War of Righteousness, the defeat at Gelnumbria Moors) would only damage his campaign for the Imperial Crown.

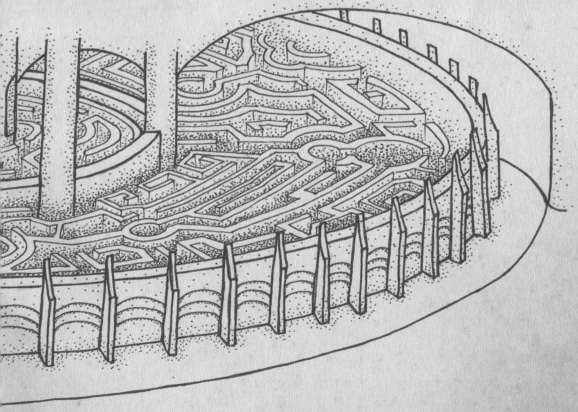

Glories and Laments Among the Ayleid Ruins

by Alexandre Hetrard

aving arrived at Gottlesfont Priory, halfway on the Gold Road between Skingrad and the Imperial City, I resolved to make a side trip to view the magnificent ruins of Ceyatatar, or "Shadow of the Fatherwoods" in the ancient Ayleid tongue. After many hours of difficult travel through tangled hawthorn hells and limberlosts, I was suddenly struck dumb by the aspect of five pure white columns rising from a jade-green mound of vines to perfect V-shaped arches and graceful capitals towering above the verdant forest growth. This spectacle caused me to meditate on the lost glories of the past, and the melancholy fate of high civilizations now poking like splinter shards of bone from the green-grown tumulus of time-swept obscurity.

Within the forest tangle I discovered an entrance leading down into the central dome of a great underground edifice once dedicated to Magnus, the God of Sight, Light, and Insight. Dimly lit by the faded power of its magical pools, the shattered white walls of the enclosure shimmered with a cold blue light.

The marble benches of the central plaza faced out across the surrounding waters to tall columns and sharp arches supporting the high dome. From the central island, stately bridges spanned the still pools to narrow walkways behind the columns, with broad vaulted avenues and limpid canals leading away through ever-deeping gloom into darkness. Reflected in the pools were the tumbled columns, collapsed walls, and riotous root and vine growth thriving the dark half-light of the magical fountains.

The ancient Ayleids recognized not the four elements of modern natural philosophy — earth, water, air, and fire — but the four elements of High Elf religion — earth, water, air, and light. The Ayleids considered fire to be but a weak and corrupt form of light, which Ayleid philosophers identified with primary magical principles. Thus their ancient subterranean temples and sanctuaries were lit by lamps, globes, pools, and fountains of purest magic.

It was by these ancient, faded, but still active magics that I knelt and contemplated the departed glories of the long-dead Ayleid architects. Gazing through the glass-smooth reflections of the surrounding pools, I could see, deep below, the slow pulse, the waxing and waning of the Welkynd stones.

The chiefest perils of these ruins to the explorer are the cunning and deadly mechanisms devised by the Ayleids to torment and confound those would invade their underground sanctuaries. What irony that after these many years, these devices should still stand vigilant against those who would admire the works of the Ayleids. For it is clear... these devices were crafted in vain. They did not secure the Ayleids against their true enemies, which were not the slaves who revolted and overthrew their cruel masters, nor the were they the savage beast peoples who learned the crafts of war and magic from their Ayleid masters. No, it was the arrogant pride of their achievements, their smug self-assurance that their empire would last forever, that doomed them to fail and fade into obscurity.

2920: The Last Year of the First Era

by Carlovac Townway

Book One: Morning Star

1 Morning Star, 2920
Mournhold, Morrowind

Almalexia lay in her bed of fur, dreaming. Not until the sun burned through her window, infusing the light wood and flesh colors of her chamber in a milky glow did she open her eyes. It was quiet and serene, a stunning reverse of the flavor of her dreams, so full of blood and celebration. For a few moments, she simply stared at the ceiling, trying to sort through her visions.

In the courtyard of her palace was a boiling pool which steamed in the coolness of the winter morning. At the wave of her hand, it cleared and she saw the face and form of her lover Vivec in his study to the north. She did not want to speak right away: he looked so handsome in his dark red robes, writing his poetry as he did every morning.

"Vivec," she said, and he raised his head in a smile, looking at her face across thousands of miles. "I have seen a vision of the end of the war."

"After eighty years, I don't think anyone can imagine an end," said Vivec with a smile, but he grew serious, trusting Almalexia's prophecies. "Who will win? Morrowind or the Cyrodilic Empire?"

"Without Sotha Sil in Morrowind , we will lose," she replied.

"My intelligence tells me the Empire will strike us to the north in early springtide, by First Seed at the latest. Could you go to Artaeum and convince him to return?"

"I'll leave tomorrow," she said, simply.

4 Morning Star, 2920
Gideon, Black Marsh

The Empress paced around her cell. Wintertide gave her wasteful energy, while in the summer she would merely sit by her window and be grateful for each breath of stale swamp wind that came to cool her. Across the room, her unfinished tapestry of a dance at the Imperial Court seemed to mock her. She ripped it from its frame, tearing the pieces apart as they drifted to the floor.

Then she laughed at her own useless gesture of defiance. She would have plenty of time to repair it and craft a hundred more. The Emperor had locked her up in Castle Giovesse seven years ago, and would likely keep her here until he or she died.

With a sigh, she pulled the cord to call her knight, Zuuk. He appeared at the door

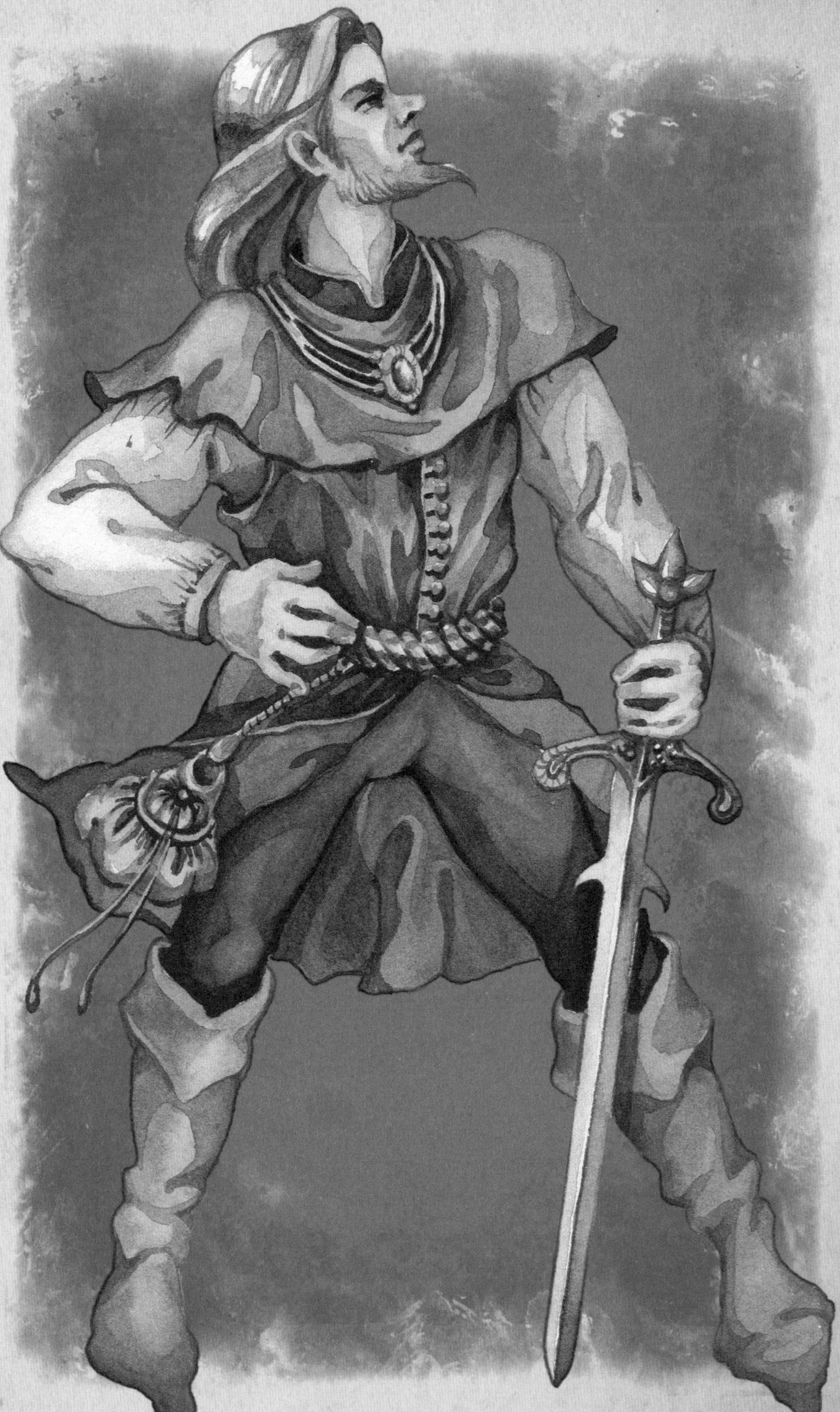

within minutes, fully uniformed as befitted an Imperial Guard. Most of the native Kothringi tribesmen of Black Marsh preferred to go about naked, but Zuuk had taken a positive delight to fashion. His silver, reflective skin was scarcely visible, only on his face, neck, and hands.

"Your Imperial Highness," he said with a bow.

"Zuuk," said Empress Tavia. "I'm bored. Lets discuss methods of assassinating my husband today."

14 Morning Star, 2920

The Imperial City , Cyrodiil

The chimes proclaiming South Wind's Prayer echoed through the wide boulevards and gardens of the Imperial City, calling all to their temples. TheEmperor Reman III always attended a service at the Temple of the One, while his son and heir Prince Juilek found it more political to attend a service at a different temple for each religious holiday. This year, it was at the cathedral Benevolence of Mara.

The Benevolence 's services were mercifully short, but it was not until well after noon that the Emperor was able to return to the palace. By then, the arena combatants were impatiently waiting for the start of the ceremony. The crowd was far less restless, as the Potentate Versidue-Shaie had arranged for a demonstration from a troupe of Khajiiti acrobats.

"Your religion is so much more convenient than mine," said the Emperor to his Potentate by way of an apology. "What is the first game?"

"A one-on-one battle between two able warriors," said the Potentate, his scaly skin catching the sun as he rose. "Armed befitting their culture."

"Sounds good," said the Emperor and clapped his hands. "Let the sport commence!"

As soon as he saw the two warriors enter the arena to the roar of the crowd, Emperor Reman III remembered that he had agreed to this several months before and forgotten about it. One combatant was the Potentate's son, Savirien-Chorak, a glistening ivory-yellow eel, gripping his katana andwakizashi with his thin, deceptively weak looking arms. The other was the Emperor's son, Prince Juilek , in Ebony armor with a savage Orcish helm,shield and longsword at his side.

"This will be fascinating to watch," hissed the Potentate, a wide grin across his narrow face. "I don't know if I've even seen a Cyrodiil fight an Akavirlike this. Usually it's army against army. At last we can settle which philosophy is better — to create armor to combat swords as your people do, or to create swords to combat armor as mine do."

No one in the crowd, aside from a few scattered Akaviri counselors and the Potentate himself wanted Savirien-Chorak to win, but there was a collective intake of breath at the sight of his graceful movements. His swords seemed to be a part of him, a tail coming from his arms to match the one behind him. It was a trick of counterbalance, allowing the young serpent man to roll up into a circle and spin into the center of the ring in offensive position. The Prince had to plod forward the less impressive traditional way.

As they sprang at each other, the crowd bellowed with delight. The Akaviri was like a moon in orbit around the Prince, effortlessly springing over his shoulder to attempt a blow from behind, but the Prince whirled around quickly to block with his shield. His counter-strike met only air as his foe fell flat to the ground and slithered between his legs, tripping him. The Prince fell to the ground with a resounding crash.

Metal and air melted together as Savirien-Chorak rained strike after strike upon the Prince, who blocked every one with his shield.

"We don't have shields in our culture," murmured Versidue-Shaie to the Emperor. "It seems strange to my boy, I imagine. In our country, if you don't want to get hit, you move out of the way."

When Savirien-Chorak was rearing back to begin another series of blinding attacks, the Prince kicked at his tail, sending him falling back momentarily. In an instant, he had rebounded, but the Prince was also back on his feet. The two circled one another, until the snake man spun forward, katana extended. The Prince saw his foe's plan, and blocked the katana with his longsword and the wakizashi with his shield. Its short punching blade impaled itself in the metal, and Savirien-Chorak was thrown off balance.

The Prince's longblade slashed across the Akavir's chest and the sudden, intense pain caused him to drop both his weapons. In a moment, it was over. Savirien-Chorak was prostate in the dust with the Prince's longsword at his throat.

"The game's over!" shouted the Emperor, barely heard over the applause from the stadium.

The Prince grinned and helped Savirien-Chorak up and over to a healer. The Emperor clapped his Potentate on the back, feeling relieved. He had not realized when the fight had begun how little chance he had given his son at victory.

"He will make a fine warrior," said Versidue-Shaie. "And a great emperor."

"Just remember," laughed the Emperor. "You Akaviri have a lot of showy moves, but if just one of our strikes comes through, it's all over for you."

"Oh, I'll remember that," nodded the Potentate.

Reman thought about that comment for the rest of the games, and had trouble fully enjoying himself. Could the Potentate be another enemy, just as the Empress had turned out to be? The matter would bear watching.

21 Morning Star, 2920
Mournhold, Morrowind

"Why don't you wear that green gown I gave you?" asked the Duke of Mournhold, watching the young maiden put on her clothes.

"It doesn't fit," smiled Turala. "And you know I like red."

"It doesn't fit because you're getting fat," laughed the Duke, pulling her down on the bed, kissing her breasts and the pouch of her stomach. She laughed at the tickles, but pulled herself up, wrapping her red robe around her.

"I'm round like a woman should be," said Turala. "Will I see you tomorrow?"

"No," said the Duke. "I must entertain Vivec tomorrow, and the next day the Duke of Ebonheart is coming. Do you know, I never really appreciated Almalexia and her political skills until she left?"

"It is the same with me," smiled Turala. "You will only appreciate me when I'm gone."

"That's not true at all," snorted the Duke. "I appreciate you now."

Turala allowed the Duke one last kiss before she was out the door. She kept thinking about what he said. Would he appreciate her more or less when he knew that she was getting fat because she was carrying his child? Would he appreciate her enough to marry her?

Book Two: Sun's Dawn

3 Sun's Dawn, 2920
The Isle of Artaeum, Summerset

otha Sil watched the init iates float one by one up to the oassom tree, taking a fruit or a flower from its high branches before dropping back to the ground with varying degrees of grace. He took a moment while nodding his head in approval to admire the day. The whitewashed statue of Syrabane, which the great mage was said to have posed for in ancient days, stood at the precipice of the cliff overlooking the bay. Pale purple proscato flowers waved to and fro in the gentle breeze. Beyond, ocean, and the misty border between Artaeum and the main island of Summurset.

"By and large, acceptable," he proclaimed as the last student dropped her fruit in his hand. With a wave of his hand, the fruit and flowers were back in the tree. With another wave, the students had formed into position in a semicircle around the sorcerer. He pulled a small fibrous ball, about a foot in diameter from his white robes.

"What is this?"

The students understood this test. It asked them to cast a spell of identification on the mysterious object. Each initiate closed his or her eyes and imagined the ball in the realm of the universal Truth. Its energy had a unique resonance as all physical and spiritual matter does, a negative aspect, a duplicate version, relative paths, true meaning, a song in the cosmos, a texture in the fabric of space, a facet of being that has always existed and always will exist.

"A ball," said a young Nord named Welleg, which brought giggles from some of the younger initiates, but a frown from most, including Sotha Sil.

"If you must be stupid, at least be amusing," growled the sorcerer, and then looked at a young, dark-haired Altmer lass who looked confused. "Lilatha, do you know?"

"It's grom," said Lilatha, uncertainly. "What the dreugh meff after they've k-k-kr-krevinasim."

"Karvinasim, but very good, nonetheless," said Sotha Sil. "Now, tell me, what does that mean?"

"I don't know," admitted Lilatha. The rest of the students also shook their heads.

"There are layers to understanding all things," said Sotha Sil. "The common man looks at an object and fits it into a place in his way of thinking. Those skilled in the Old Ways, in the way of the Psijic, in Mysticism, can see an object and identify it by its proper role. But one more layer is needed to be peeled back to achieve understanding. You must identify the object by its role and its truth and interpret that meaning. In this case, this ball is indeed grom, which is a substance created by the dreugh, an underwater race in the north and western parts of the continent. For one year of their life, they undergo karvinasim when they walk upon the land. Following that, they return to the water and meff, or devour the skin and organs they needed for land-dwelling. Then they vomit it up into little balls like this. Grom. Dreugh vomit."

The students looked at the ball a little queasily. Sotha Sil always loved this lesson.

4 Sun's Dawn, 2920
The Imperial City, Cyrodiil

"Spies," muttered the Emperor, sitting in his bath, staring at a lump on his foot. "All around me, traitors and spies."

His mistress Rijja washed his back, her legs wrapped around his waist. She knew after all these many years when to be sensual and when to be sexual. When he was in a mood like this, it was best to be calmly, soothingly, seductively sensual. And not to say a word unless he asked her a direct question.

Which he did: "What do you think when a fellow steps on his Imperial Majesty's foot and says 'I'm sorry, Your Imperial Majesty'? Don't you think 'Pardon me, Your Imperial Majesty' is more appropriate? 'I'm sorry,' well that almost sounds like the bastard Argonian was sorry I am his Imperial Majesty. That he hopes we lose the war with Morrowind, that's what it sounds like."

"What would make you feel better?" asked Rijja. "Would you like him flogged? He is only, as you say, the Battlechief of Soulrest. It would teach him to mind where he's stepping."

"My father would have flogged him. My grandfather would have had him killed," the Emperor grumbled. "But I don't mind if they all step on my feet, provided they respect me. And don't plot against me."

"You must trust someone."

"Only you," smiled the Emperor, turning slightly to give Rijja a kiss. "And my son Juilek, I suppose, though I wish he were a little more cautious."

"And your council, and the Potentate?" asked Rijja.

"A pack of spies and a snake," laughed the Emperor, kissing his mistress again. As they began to make love, he whispered, "As long as you're true, I can handle the world."

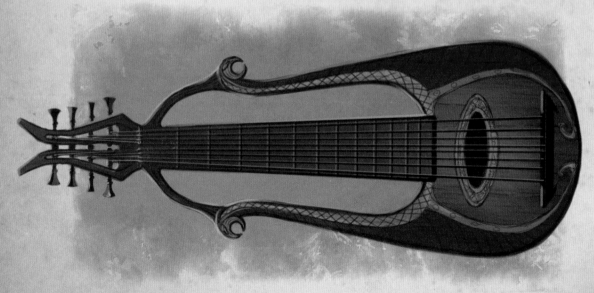

13 Sun's Dawn, 2920
Mournhold, Morrowind

Turala stood at the black, bejeweled city gates. A wind howled around her, but she felt nothing.

The Duke had been furious upon hearing his favorite mistress was pregnant and cast her from his sight. She tried again and again to see him, but his guards turned her away. Finally, she returned to her family and told them the truth. If only she had lied and told them she did not know who the father was. A soldier, a wandering adventurer, anyone. But she told them that the father was the Duke, a member of the House Indoril. And they did what she knew they would have to do, as proud members of the House Redoran.

Upon her hand was burned the sign of Expulsion her weeping father had branded on her. But the Duke's cruelty hurt her far more. She looked out the gate and into the wide winter plains. Twisted, sleeping trees and skies without birds. No one in Morrowind would take her in now. She must go far away.

With slow, sad steps, she began her journey.

16 Sun's Dawn, 2920
Senchal, Anequina (modern day Elsweyr)

"What troubles you?" asked Queen Hasaama, noticing her husband's sour mood. At the end of most Lovers' Days he was in an excellent mood, dancing in the ballroom with all the guests, but tonight he retired early. When she found him, he was curled in the bed, frowning.

"That blasted bard's tale about Polydor and Eloisa put me in a rotten state," he growled. "Why did he have to be so depressing?"

"But isn't that the truth of the tale, my dear? Weren't they doomed because of the cruel nature of the world?"

"It doesn't matter what the truth is, he did a rotten job of telling a rotten tale, and I'm not going to let him do it anymore," King Dro'Zel sprang from the bed. His eyes were rheumy with tears. "Where did they say he was from again?"

"I believe Gilverdale in easternmost Valenwood," said the Queen, shaken. "My husband, what are you going to do?" Dro'Zel was out of the room in a single spring, bounding up the stairs to his tower. If Queen Hasaama knew what her husband was going to do, she did not try to stop him. He had been erratic of late, prone to fits and even occasional seizures. But she never suspected the depths of his madness, and his loathing for the bard and his tale of the wickedness and perversity found in mortal man.

19 Sun's Dawn, 2920
Gilverdale, Valenwood

"Listen to me again," said the old carpenter. "If cell three holds worthless brass, then cell two holds the gold key. If cell one holds the gold key, then cell three hold worthless brass. If cell two holds worthless brass, then cell one holds the gold key."

"I understand," said the lady. "You told me. And so cell one holds the gold key, right?"

"No," said the carpenter. "Let me start from the top."

"Mama?" said the little boy, pulling on his mother's sleeve.

"Just one moment, dear, mother's talking," she said, concentrating on the riddle. "You said 'cell three holds the golden key if cell two holds worthless brass,' right?"

"No," said the carpenter patiently. "Cell three holds worthless brass, if cell two ——"

"Mama!" cried the boy. His mother finally looked.

A bright red mist was pouring over the town in a wave, engulfing building after building in its wake. Striding before was a red-skinned giant. TheDaedra Molag Bal. He was smiling.

29 Sun's Dawn, 2920
Gilverdale, Valenwood

Almalexia stopped her steed in the vast moor of mud to let him drink from the river. He refused to, even seemed repelled by the water. It struck her as odd: they had been making excellent time from Mournhold, and surely he must be thirsty. She dismounted and joined her retinue.

"Where are we now?" she asked.

One of her ladies pulled out a map. "I thought we were approaching a town called Gilverdale."

Almalexia closed her eyes and opened them again quickly. The vision was too much to bear. As her followers watched, she picked up a piece of brick and a fragment of bone, and clutched them to her heart.

"We must continue on to Artaeum," she said quietly.

The Year continues in First Seed.

Book Three: First Seed

The Last Year of the First Era

15 First Seed, 2920
Caer Suvio, Cyrodiil

From their vantage point high in the hills, the Emperor Reman III could still see the spires of the Imperial City, but he knew he was far away from hearth and home. Lord Glavius had a luxurious villa, but it was not close to being large enough to house the entire army within its walls. Tents lined the hillsides, and the soldiers were flocking to enjoy his lordship's famous hot springs. Little wonder: winter chill still hung in the air.

"Prince Juilek, your son, is not feeling well."

When Potentate Versidue-Shaie spoke, the Emperor jumped. How that Akavir could slither across the grass without making a sound was a mystery to him.

"Poisoned, I'd wager," grumbled Reman. "See to it he gets a healer. I told him to hire a taster like I have, but the boy's headstrong. There are spies all around us, I know it."

"I believe you're right, your imperial majesty," said Versidue-Shaie. "These are treacherous times, and we must take precautions to see that Morrowind does not win this war, either on the field or by more insidious means. That is why I would suggest that you not lead the vanguard into battle. I know you would want to, as your illustrious ancestors Reman I, Brazollus Dor, and Reman II did, but I fear it would be foolhardy. I hope you do not mind me speaking frankly like this."

"No," nodded Reman. "I think you're right. Who would lead the vanguard then?"

"I would say Prince Juilek, if he were feeling better," replied the Akavir. "Failing that, Storig of Farrun, with Queen Naghea of Riverhold at left flank, and Warchief Ulaqth of Lilmoth at right flank."

"A Khajiit at left flank and an Argonian at right," frowned the Emperor. "I never do trust beastfolk."

The Potentate took no offense. He knew that "beastfolk" referred to the natives of Tamriel, not to the Tsaesci of Akavir like himself. "I quite agree your imperial majesty, but you must agree that they hate the Dunmer. Ulaqth has a particular grudge after all the slave-raids on his lands by the Duke of Mournhold."

The Emperor conceded it was so, and the Potentate retired. It was surprising, thought Reman, but for the first time, the Potentate seemed trustworthy. He was a good man to have on one's side.

18 First Seed, 2920
Ald Erfoud, Morrowind

"How far is the Imperial Army?" asked Vivec.

"Two days' march," replied his lieutenant. "If we march all night tonight, we can get higher ground at the Pryai tomorrow morning. Our intelligence tells us the Emperor will be commanding the rear, Storig of Farrun has the vanguard, Naghea of Riverhold at left flank, and Ulaqth of Lilmoth at right flank."

"Ulaqth," whispered Vivec, an idea forming. "Is this intelligence reliable? Who brought it to us?"

"A Breton spy in the Imperial Army," said the lieutenant and gestured towards a young, sandy-haired man who stepped forward and bowed to Vivec.

"What is your name and why is a Breton working for us against the Cyrodiils?" asked Vivec, smiling.

"My name is Cassyr Whitley of Dwynnen," said the man. "And I am working for you because not everyone can say he spied for a god. And I understood it would be, well, profitable."

Vivec laughed, "It will be, if your information is accurate."

19 First Seed, 2920
Bodrum, Morrowind

The quiet hamlet of Bodrum looked down on the meandering river, the Pryai. It was an idyllic site, lightly wooded where the water took the bend around a steep bluff to the east with a gorgeous wildflower meadow to the west. The strange flora of Morrowind met the strange flora of Cyrodiil on the border and commingled gloriously.

"There will be time to sleep when you've finished!"

The soldiers had been hearing that all morning. It was not enough that they had been marching all night, now they were chopping down trees on the bluff and damming the river so its waters spilled over. Most of them had reached the point where they were too tired to complain about being tired.

"Let me be certain I understand, my lord," said Vivec's lieutenant. "We take the bluff so we can fire arrows and spells down on them from above. That's why we need all the trees cleared out. Damming the river floods the plain below so they'll be trudging through mud, which should hamper their movement."

"That's exactly half of it," said Vivec approvingly. He grabbed a nearby soldier who was hauling off the trees. "Wait, I need you to break off the straightest, strongest branches of the trees and whittle them into spears. If you recruit a hundred or so others, it won't take you more than a few hours to make all we need."

The soldier wearily did as he was bade. The men and women got to work, fashioning spears from the trees.

"If you don't mind me asking," said the lieutenant. "The soldiers don't need any more weapons. They're too tired to hold the ones they've got."

"These spears aren't for holding," said Vivec and whispered, "If we tired them out today, they'll get a good night's sleep tonight" before he got to work supervising their work.

It was essential that they be sharp, of course, but equally important that they be well balanced and tapered proportionally. The perfect point for stability was a pyramid, not the conical point of some lances and spears. He had the men hurl the spears they had completed to test their strength, sharpness, and balance, forcing them to begin on a new one if they broke. Gradually, out of sheer exhaustion from doing it wrong, the men learned how to create the perfect wooden spears. Once they were through, he showed them how they were to be arranged and where.

That night, there was no drunken pre-battle carousing, and no nervous neophytes stayed up worrying about the battle to come. As soon as the sun sank beneath the wooded hills, the camp was at rest, but for the sentries.

20 First Seed, 2920
Bodrum, Morrowind

Miramor was exhausted. For last six days, he had gambled and whored all night and then marched all day. He was looking forward to the battle, but even more than that, he was looking forward to some rest afterwards. He was in the Emperor's command at the rear flank, which was good because it seemed unlikely that he would be killed. On the other hand, it meant traveling over the mud and waste the army ahead left in their wake.

As they began the trek through the wildflower field, Miramor and all the soldiers around him sank ankle-deep in cold mud. It was an effort to even keep moving. Far, far up ahead, he could see the vanguard of the army led by Lord Storig emerging from the meadow at the base of a bluff.

That was when it all happened.

An army of Dunmer appeared above the bluff like rising Daedra, pouring fire and floods of arrows down on the vanguard. Simultaneously, a company of men bearing the flag of the Duke of Mournhold galloped around the shore, disappearing along the shallow river's edge where it dipped to a timbered glen to the east. Warchief Ulaqth nearby on the right flank let out a bellow of revenge at the sight and gave chase. Queen Naghea sent her flank towards the embankment to the west to intercept the army on the bluff.

The Emperor could think of nothing to do. His troops were too bogged down to move forward quickly and join the battle. He ordered them to face east towards the timber, in case Mournhold's company was trying to circle around through the woods. They never came out, but many men, facing west, missed the battle entirely. Miramor kept his eyes on the bluff.

A tall Dunmer he supposed must have been Vivec gave a signal, and the battlemages cast their spells at something to the west. From what transpired, Miramor deduced it was a dam. A great torrent of water spilled out, washing Naghea's left flank into the remains of the vanguard and the two together down river to the east.

The Emperor paused, as if waiting for his vanquished army to return, and then called a retreat. Miramor hid in the rushes until they had passed by and then waded as quietly as he could to the bluff.

The Morrowind army was retiring as well back to their camp. He could hear them celebrating above him as he padded along the shore. To the east, he saw the Imperial Army. They had been washed into a net of spears strung across the river, Naghea's left flank on Storig's vanguard on Ulaqth's right flank, bodies of hundreds of soldiers strung together like beads.

Miramor took whatever valuables he could carry from the corpses and then ran down the river. He had to go many miles before the water was clear again, unpolluted by blood.

29 First Seed, 2920

Hegathe, Hammerfell

"You have a letter from the Imperial City," said the chief priestess, handing the parchment to Corda. All the young priestesses smiled and made faces of astonishment, but the truth was that Corda's sister Rijja wrote very often, at least once a month.

Corda took the letter to the garden to read it, her favorite place, an oasis in the monochromatic sand-colored world of the conservatorium The letter itself was nothing unusual: filled with court gossip, the latest fashions which were tending to winedark velvets, and reports of the Emperor's ever-growing paranoia.

"You are so lucky to be away from all of this," wrote Rijja. "The Emperor is convinced that his latest battlefield fiasco is all a result of spies in the palace. He has even taken to questioning me. Ruptga keep it so you never have a life as interesting as mine."

Corda listened to the sounds of the desert and prayed to Ruptga the exact opposite wish.

Book Four: Rain's Hand

3 Rain's Hand, 2920
Coldharbour, Oblivion

otha Sil proceeded as quickly as he could through the blackened halls of the palace, half-submerged in brackish water. All around him, nasty gelatinous creatures scurried into the reeds, bursts of white fire lit up the upper arches of the hall before disappearing, and smells assaulted him, rancid death one moment, sweet flowered perfume the next. Several times he had visited the Daedra princes in their Oblivion, but every time, something different awaited him.

He knew his purpose, and refused to be distracted.

Eight of the more prominent Daedra princes were awaiting him in the half-melted, domed room. Azura, Prince of Dusk and Dawn; Boethiah, Prince of Plots; Hermaeus Mora, Daedra of Knowledge; Hircine, the Hunter; Malacath, God of Curses; Mehrunes Dagon, Prince of Disaster; Molag Bal, Prince of Rage; Sheogorath, the Mad One.

Above them, the sky cast tormented shadows upon the meeting.

5 Rain's Hand, 2920
The Isle of Artaeum, Summurset

Sotha Sil's voice cried out, echoing from the cave, "Move the rock!"

Immediately, the initiates obeyed, rolling aside the great boulder that blocked the entrance to the Dreaming Cave. Sotha Sil emerged, his face smeared with ash, weary. He felt he had been away for months, years, but only a few days had transpired. Lilatha took his arm to help him walk, but he refused her help with a kind smile and a shake of his head.

"Were you ... successful?" she asked.

"The Daedra princes I spoke with have agreed to our terms," he said flatly. "Disasters such as befell Gilverdale should be averted. Only through certain intermediaries such as witches or sorcerers will they answer the call of man and mer."

"And what did you promise them in return?" asked the Nord boy Welleg.

"The deals we make with Daedra," said Sotha Sil, continuing on to Iachesis' palace to meet with the Master of the Psijic Order. "Should not be discussed with the innocent."

8 Rain's Hand, 2920
The Imperial City, Cyrodiil

A storm billeted the windows of the Prince's bedchamber, bringing a smell of moist air to mix with the censors filled with burning incense and herbs.

"A letter has arrived from the Empress, your mother," said the courier. "Anxiously inquiring after your health."

"What frightened parents I have!" laughed Prince Juilek from his bed.

"It is only natural for a mother to worry," said Savirien-Chorak, the Potentate's son.

"There is everything unnatural about my family, Akavir. My exiled mother fears that my father will imagine me of being a traitor, covetous of the crown, and is having me poisoned," the Prince sank back into his pillow, annoyed. "The Emperor has insisted on me having a taster for all my meals as he does."

"There are many plots," agreed the Akavir. "You have been abed for nearly three weeks with every healer in the empire shuffling through like a slow ballroom dance. At least, all can see that you're getting stronger."

"Strong enough to lead the vanguard against Morrowind soon, I hope," said Juilek.

11 Rain's Hand, 2920
The Isle of Artaeum, Summurset

The initiates stood quietly in a row along the arbor loggia, watching the long, deep, marble-lined trench ahead of them flash with fire. The air above it vibrated with the waves of heat. Though each student kept his or her face sturdy and emotionless, as a true Psijic should, their terror was nearly as palpable as the heat. Sotha Sil closed his eyes and uttered the charm of fire resistance. Slowly, he walked across the basin of leaping flames, climbing to the other side, unscathed. Not even his white robe had been burned.

"The charm is intensified by the energy you bring to it, by your own skills, just as all spells are," he said. "Your imagination and your willpower are the keys. There is no need for a spell to give you a resistance to air, or a resistance to flowers, and after you cast the charm, you must forget there is even a need for a spell to give you resistance to fire. Do not confuse what I am saying: resistance is not about ignoring the fire's reality. You will feel the substance of flame, the texture of it, its hunger, and even the heat of it, but you will know that it will not hurt or injure you."

The students nodded and one by one, they cast the spell and made the walk through the fire. Some even went so far as to bend over and scoop up a handful of fire and feed it air, so it expanded like a bubble and melted through their fingers. Sotha Sil smiled. They were fighting their fear admirably.

The Chief Proctor Thargallith came running from the arbor arches, "Sotha Sil! Almalexia arrived on Artaeum. Iachesis told me to fetch you."

Sotha Sil turned to Thargallith for only a moment, but he knew instantly from the screams what had transpired. The Nord lad Wellig had not cast the spell properly and was burning. The smell of scorched hair and flesh panicked the other students who were struggling to get out of the basin, pulling him with them, but the incline was too steep away from the entry points. With a wave of his hand, Sotha Sil extinguished the flame.

Wellig and several other students were burned, but not badly. The sorcerer cast a healing spell on them, before turning back to Thargallith.

"I'll be with you in a moment, and give Almalexia the time to shake the road dust from her train," Sotha Sil turned back to the students, his voice flat. "Fear does not break spells, but doubt and incompetence are the great enemies of any spellcaster. Master Welleg, you will pack your bags. I'll arrange for a boat to bring you to the mainland tomorrow morning."

The sorcerer found Almalexia and Iachesis in the study, drinking hot tea, and laughing. She was more beautiful than he had remembered, though he had never before seen her so disheveled, wrapped in a blanket, dangling her damp long black tresses before the fire to dry. At Sotha Sil's approach, she leapt to her feet and embraced him.

"Did you swim all the way from Morrowind?" he smiled.

"It's pouring rain from Skywatch down to the coast," she explained, returning his smile.

"Only a half a league away, and it never rains here," said Iachesis proudly. "Of course, I sometimes miss the excitement of Summurset, and sometimes even the mainland itself. Still, I'm always very impressed by anyone out there who gets anything accomplished. It is a world of distractions. Speaking of distractions, what's all this I hear about a war?"

"You mean the one that's been bloodying the continent for the last eighty years, Master?" asked Sotha Sil, amused.

"I suppose that's the one I mean," said Iachesis with a shrug of his shoulders. "How is that war going?"

"We will lose it, unless I can convince Sotha Sil to leave Artaeum," said Almalexia, losing her smile. She had meant to wait and talk to her friend in private, but the old Altmer gave her courage to press on. "I have had visions; I know it to be true."

Sotha Sil was silent for a moment, and then looked at Iachesis, "I must return to Morrowind."

"Knowing you, if you must do something, you will," sighed the old Master. "The Psijics' way is not to be distracted. Wars are fought, Empires rise and fall. You must go, and so must we."

"What do you mean, Iachesis? You're leaving the island?"

"No, the island will be leaving the sea," said Iachesis, his voice taking on a dreamy quality. "In a few years, the mists will move over Artaeum and we will be gone. We are counselors by nature, and there are too many counselors in Tamriel as it is. No, we will go, and return when the land needs us again, perhaps in another age."

The old Altmer struggles to his feet, and drained the last sip of his drink before leaving Sotha Sil and Almalexia alone: "Don't miss the last boat."

Book Five: Second Seed

5 Second Seed, 2920

The Imperial City, Cyrodiil

"Your Imperial Majesty," said the Potentate Versidue-Shaie, opening the door to his chamber with a smile. "I have not seen you lately. I thought perhaps you were ... indisposed with the lovely Rijja."

"She's taking the baths at Mir Corrup," the Emperor Reman III said miserably.

"Please, come in."

"I've reached the stage where I can only trust three people: you, my son the Prince, and Rijja," said the Emperor petulantly. "My entire council is nothing but a pack of spies."

"What seems to be the matter, your imperial majesty?" asked the Potentate Versidue-Shaie sympathetically, drawing closed the thick curtain in his chamber. Instantly all sound outside the room was extinguished, echoing footsteps in the marble halls and birds in the springtide gardens. "I've discovered that a notorious poisoner, an Orma tribeswoman from Black Marsh called Catchica, was with the army at Caer Suvio while we were encamped there when my son was poisoned, before the Battle at Bodrum. I'm sure she would have preferred to kill me, but the opportunity didn't present itself," The Emperor fumed. "The Council suggests that we need evidence of her involvement before we prosecute."

"Of course they would," said the Potentate thoughtfully. "Particularly if one or more of them was in on the plot. I have a thought, your imperial majesty."

"Yes?" said Reman impatiently. "Out with it!"

"Tell the Council you're dropping the matter, and I will send out the Guard to track this Catchica down and follow her. We will see who her friends are, and perhaps get an idea of the scope of this plot on your imperial majesty's life."

"Yes," said Reman with a satisfied frown. "That's a capital plan. We will track this scheme to whomever it leads to."

"Decidedly, your imperial majesty," smiled the Potentate, parting the curtain so the Emperor could leave. In the hallway outside was Potentate Versidue-Shaie's son, Savirien-Chorak. The boy bowed to the Emperor before entering the Potentate's chamber.

"Are you in trouble, father?" whispered the Akaviri lad. "I heard the Emperor found out about whatshername, the poisoner."

"The great art of Speechcraft, my boy," said Versidue-Shaie to his son. "Is to tell them what they want to hear in a way that gets them to do what you want them to do. I need you to get a letter to Catchica, and make certain that she understands that if she does not follow the instructions perfectly, she is risking her own life more than ours."

13 Second Seed, 2920
Mir Corrup, Cyrodiil

Rijja sank luxuriantly into the burbling hot spring, feeling her skin tingle like it was being rubbed by millions of little stones. The rock shelf over her head sheltered her from the misting rain, but let all the sunshine in, streaming in layers through the branches of the trees. It was an idyllic moment in an idyllic life, and when she was finished she knew that her beauty would be entirely restored. The only thing she needed was a drink of water. The bath itself, while wonderfully fragrant, tasted always of chalk.

"Water!" she cried to her servants. "Water, please!"

A gaunt woman with rags tied over her eyes ran to her side and dropped a goatskin of water. Rijja was about to laugh at the woman's prudery — she herself was not ashamed of her naked body — but then she noticed through a crease in the rags that the old woman had no eyes at all. She was like one of those Orma tribesmen Rijja had heard about, but never met. Born without eyes, they were masters of their other senses. The Lord of Mir Corrup hired very exotic servants, she thought to herself.

In a moment, the woman was gone and forgotten. Rijja found it very hard to concentrate on anything but the sun and the water. She opened the cork, but the liquid within had a strange, metallic smell to it. Suddenly, she was aware that she was not alone.

"Lady Rijja," said the captain of the Imperial Guard. "You are, I see, acquainted with Catchica?"

"I've never heard of her," stammered Rijja before becoming indignant. "What are you doing here? This body is not for your leering eyes."

"Never heard of her, when we saw her with you not a minute ago," said the captain, picking up the goatskin and smelling it. "Brought you neivous ichor, did she? To poison the Emperor with?"

"Captain," said one of the guards, running up to him quickly. "We cannot find the Argonian. It is as if she disappeared into the woods."

"Yes, they're good at that," said the captain. "No matter though. We've got her contact at court. That should please his Imperial Majesty. Seize her."

As the guards pulled the writhing naked woman from the pool, she screamed, "I'm innocent! I don't know what this is all about, but I've done nothing! The Emperor will have your heads for this!"

"Yes, I imagine he will," smiled the captain. "If he trusts you."

21 Second Seed, 2920
Gideon, Black Marsh

The Sow and Vulture tavern was the sort of out-of-the-way place that Zuuk favored for these sorts of interviews. Besides himself and his companion, there were only a couple of old seadogs in the shadowy room, and they were more unconscious from drink than aware. The grime of the unwashed floor was something you felt rather than saw. Copious dust hung in the air unmoving in the sparse rays of dying sunlight.

"You have experience in heavy combat?" asked Zuuk. "The reward is good for this assignment, but the risks are great as well."

"Certainly I have combat experience," replied Miramor haughtily. "I was at the Battle of Bodrum just two months ago. If you do your part and get the Emperor to ride through Dozsa Pass with a minimal escort on the day and the time we've discussed, I'll do my part. Just be certain that he's not traveling in disguise. I'm not going to slaughter every caravan that passes through in the hopes that it contains Emperor Reman."

Zuuk smiled, and Miramor looked at himself in the Kothringi's reflective face. He liked the way he looked: the consummate confident professional.

"Agreed," said Zuuk. "And then you shall have the rest of your gold."

Zuuk placed the large chest onto the table between them. He stood up.

"Wait a few minutes before leaving," said Zuuk. "I don't want you following me. Your employers wish to maintain their anonymity, if by chance you are caught and tortured."

"Fine by me," said Miramor, ordering more grog.

Zuuk rode his mount through the cramped labyrinthine streets of Gideon, and both he and his horse were happy to pass through the gates into the country. The main road to Castle Giovese was flooded as it was every year in springtide, but Zuuk knew a shorter way over the hills. Riding fast under trees drooping with moss and treacherous slime-coated rocks, he arrived at the castle gates in two hours' time. He wasted no time in climbing to Tavia's cell at the top of the highest tower.

"What did you think of him?" asked the Empress.

"He's a fool," replied Zuuk. "But that's what we want for this sort of assignment."

30 Second Seed, 2920
Thurzo Fortress, Cyrodiil

Rijja screamed and screamed and screamed. Within her cell, her only audience was the giant gray stones, crusted with moss but still sturdy. The guards outside were deaf to her as they were deaf to all prisoners. The Emperor, miles away in the Imperial City, had likewise been deaf to her cries of innocence.

She screamed knowing well that no one would likely hear her ever again.

31 Second Seed, 2920
Kavas Rim Pass, Cyrodiil

It had been days, weeks since Turala had seen another human face, Cyrodiil or Dunmer. As she trod the road, she thought to herself how strange it was that such an uninhabited place as Cyrodiil had become the Imperial Province, seat of an Empire. Even the Bosmer in Valenwood must have more populated forests than this Heartland wood.

She thought back. Was it a month ago, two, when she crossed the border from Morrowind into Cyrodiil? It had been much colder then, but other than that, she had no sense of time. The guards had been brusque, but as she was carrying no weaponry, they elected to let her through. Since then, she had seen a few caravans, even shared a meal with some adventurers camping for the night, but met no one who would give her a ride to a town.

Turala stripped off her shawl and dragged it behind her. For a moment, she thought she heard someone behind her and spun around. No one was there. Just a bird perched on a branch making a sound like laughter.

She walked on, and then stopped. Something was happening. The child had been kicking in her belly for some time now, but this was a different kind of spasm. With a groan, she lurched over to the side of the path, collapsing into the grass. Her child was coming.

She lay on her back and pushed, but she could barely see with her tears of pain and frustration. How had it come to this? Giving birth in the wilderness, all by herself, to a child whose father was the Duke of Mournhold? Her scream of rage and agony shook the birds from the trees

The bird that had been laughing at her earlier flew down to the road. She blinked, and the bird was gone and in its place, a naked Elf man stood, not as dark as a Dunmer, but not as pale as the Altmer. She knew at once it was an Ayleid, a Wild Elf. Turala screamed, but the man held her down. After a few minutes of struggle, she felt a release, and then fainted away.

When she awoke, it was to the sound of a baby crying. The child had been cleaned and was lying by her side. Turala picked up her baby girl, and for the first time that year, felt tears of happiness stream down her face. She whispered to the trees, "Thank you" and began walking with babe in her arms down the road to the west.

Book Six: Mid Year

2 Mid Year, 2920
Balmora, Morrowind

"The Imperial army is gathered to the south," said Cassyr. "They are a two weeks march from Ald Iuval and Lake Coronati, heavily armored."

Vivec nodded. Ald Iuval and its sister city on the other side of the lake Ald Marak were strategically important fortresses. He had been expecting a move against them for some time. His captain pulled down a map of southwestern Morrowind from the wall and smoothed it out, fighting a gentle summer sea breeze wafting in from the open window.

"They were heavily armored, you say?" asked the captain.

"Yes, sir," said Cassyr. "They were camped out near Bethal Gray in the Heartland, and I saw nothing but Ebony, Dwarven, and Daedric, fine weaponry, and siege equipment."

"How about spellcasters and boats?" asked Vivec.

"A horde of battlemages," replied Cassyr. "But no boats."

"As heavily armored as they are, it will take them at least two weeks, like you said, to get from Bethal Gray to Lake Coronati," Vivec studied the map carefully. "They'd be dragged down in the bogs if they then tried to circle around to Ald Marak from the north, so they must be planning to cross the straits here and take Ald Iuval. Then they'd proceed around the lake to the east and take Ald Marak from the south."

"They'll be vulnerable along the straits," said the captain. "Provided we strike when they are more than halfway across and can't retreat back to the Heartland."

"Your intelligence has once again served us well," said Vivec, smiling to Cassyr. "We will beat back the Imperial aggressors yet again."

3 Mid Year, 2920
Bethal Gray, Cyrodiil

"Will you be returning back this way after your victory?" asked Lord Bethal.

Prince Juilek barely paid the man any attention. He was focused on the army packing its camp. It was a cool morning in the forest, but there were no clouds. All the makings of a hot afternoon march, particularly in such heavy armor.

"If we return shortly, it will be because of defeat," said the Prince. He could see down in the meadow, the Potentate Versidue-Shaie paying his lordship's steward for the use of the village's food, wine, and whores. An army was an expensive thing, for certes.

"My Prince," said Lord Bethal with concern. "Is your army beginning a march due east? That will just lead you to the shores of Lake Coronati. You'll want to go south-east to get to the straits."

"You just make certain your merchants get their share of our ," said the Prince with a grin. "Let me worry about my army's direction."

16 Mid Year, 2920
Lake Coronati, Morrowind

Vivec stared across the blue expanse of the lake, seeing his reflection and the reflection of his army in the cool blue waters. What he did not see was the Imperial Army's reflection. They must have reached the straits by now, barring any mishaps in the forest. Tall feather-thin lake trees blocked much of his view of the straits, but an army, particularly one clan in slow-moving heavy armor could not move invisibly, silently.

"Let me see the map again," he called to his captain. "Is there no other way they could approach?"

"We have sentries posted in the swamps to the north in case they're fool enough to go there and be bogged under," said the captain. "We would at least hear about it. But there is no other way across the lake except through the straits."

Vivec looked down again at his reflection, which seemed to be distorting his image, mocking him. Then he looked back on the map.

"Spy," said Vivec, calling Cassyr over. "When you said the army had a horde of battlemages, what made you so certain they were battlemages?"

"They were wearing gray robes with mystical insignia on them," explained Cassyr. "I figured they were mages, and why else would such a vast number travel with the army? They couldn't have all been healers."

"You fool!" roared Vivec. "They're mystics schooled in the art of Alteration. They've cast a spell of water breathing on the entire army."

Vivec ran to a new vantage point where he could see the north. Across the lake, though it was but a small shadow on the horizon, they could see gouts of flame from the assault on Ald Marak. Vivec bellowed with fury and his captain got to work at once redirecting the army to circle the lake and defend the castle.

"Return to Dwynnen," said Vivec flatly to Cassyr before he rode off to join the battle. "Your services are no longer needed nor wanted."

It was already too late when the Morrowind army neared Ald Marak. It had been taken by the Imperial Army.

19 Mid Year, 2920
The Imperial City, Cyrodiil

The Potentate arrived in the Imperial City amid great fanfare, the streets lined with men and women cheering him as the symbol of the taking of Ald Marak. Truth be told, a greater number would have turned out had the Prince returned, and the Versidue-Shaie knew it. Still, it pleased him to no end. Never before had citizens of Tamriel cheered the arrival of an Akaviri into their land.

The Emperor Reman III greeted him with a warm embrace, and then tore into the letter he had brought from the Prince.

"I don't understand," he said at last, still joyous but equally confused. "You went under the lake?"

"Ald Marak is a very well-fortified fortress," explained the Potentate. "As, I might add, the army of Morrowind has rediscovered, now that they are on the outside. To take it, we had to attack by surprise and with our soldiery in the sturdiest of armor. By casting the spell that allowed us to breathe underwater, we were able to travel faster than Vivec would have guessed, the weight of the armor made less by the aquatic surroundings, and attack from the waterbound west side of the fortress where their defenses were at their weakest."

"Brilliant!" the Emperor crowed. "You are a wonderous tactician, Versidue-Shaie! If your fathers had been as good at this as you are, Tamriel would be Akaviri domain!"

The Potentate had not planned to take credit for Prince Juilek's design, but on the Emperor's reference to his people's fiasco of an invasion two hundred and sixteen years ago, he made up his mind. He smiled modestly and soaked up the praise.

21 Mid Year, 2920
Ald Marak, Morrowind

Savirien-Chorak slithered to the wall and watched through the arrow slit the Morrowind army retreating back to the forestland between the swamps and the castle grounds. It seemed like the ideal opportunity to strike. Perhaps the forests could be burned and the army within them. Perhaps with Vivec in their enemies' hands, the army would allow them possession of Ald Iuval as well. He suggested these ideas to the Prince.

"What you seem to be forgetting," laughed Prince Juilek. "Is that I gave my word that no harm to the army or to their commanders during the truce negotiations. Do you not have honor during warfare on Akavir?"

"My Prince, I was born here in Tamriel, I have never been to my people's home," replied the snake man. "But even so, your ways are strange to me. You expected no quarter and I gave you none when we fought in the Imperial Arena five months ago."

"That was a game," replied the Prince, before nodding to his steward to let the Dunmer battle chief in.

Juilek had never seen Vivec before, but he had heard he was a living god. What came before him was but a man. A powerfully built man, handsome, with an intelligent face, but a man nonetheless. The Prince was pleased: a man he could speak with, but not a god.

"Greetings, my worthy adversary," said Vivec. "We seem to be at an impasse."

"Not necessarily," said the Prince. "You don't want to give us Morrowind, and I can't fault you for that. But I must have your coastline to protect the Empire from overseas aggressions, and certain key strategic border castles, such as this one, as well as Ald Umbeil, Tel Aruhn, Ald Lambasi, and Tel Mothrivra."

"And in return?" asked Vivec.

"In return?" laughed Savirien-Chorak. "You forget we are the victors here, not you."

"In return," said Prince Juilek carefully. "There will be no Imperial attacks on Morrowind, unless in return to an attack by you. You will be protected from invaders by the Imperial navy. And your land may expand by taking certain estates in Black Marsh, whichever you choose, provided they are not needed by the Empire."

"A reasonable offer," said Vivec after a pause. "You must forgive me, I am unused to Cyrodiils who offer something in return for what they take. May I have a few days to decide?"

"We will meet again in a week's time," said the Prince, smiling. "In the meantime, if your army provokes no attacks on mine, we are at peace."

Vivec left the Prince's chamber, feeling that Almalexia was right. The war was at an end. This Prince would make an excellent Emperor.

Book Seven: Sun's Height

4 Sun's Height, 2920
The Imperial City, Cyrodiil

he Emperor Reman III and his Potentate Versidue-Shaie took a stroll around the Imperial Gardens. Studded with statuary and fountains, the north gardens fit the Emperor's mood, as well as being the coolest acreage in the City during the heat of summertide. Austere, tiered flowerbeds of blue-gray and green towered all around them as they walked.

"Vivec agreed to the Prince's terms for peace," said Reman. "My son will be returning in two weeks' time."

"This is excellent news," said the Potentate carefully. "I hope the Dunmer will honor the terms. We might have asked for more. The fortress at Black Gate, for example. But I suppose the Prince knows what is reasonable. He would not cripple the Empire just for peace."

"I have been thinking lately of Rijja and what caused her to plot against my life," said the Emperor, pausing to admire a statue of the Slave Queen Alessia before continuing. "The only thing I can think of to account for it is that she admired my son too much. She may have loved me for my power and my personality, but he, after all, is young and handsome and will one day inherit my throne. She must have thought that if I were dead, she could have an Emperor who had both youth and power."

"The Prince ... was in on this plot?" asked Versidue-Shaie. It was a difficult game to play, anticipating where the Emperor's paranoia would strike next.

"Oh, I don't think so," said Reman, smiling. "No, my son loves me well."

"Are you aware that Corda, Rijja's sister is an initiate of the Morwha conservatorium in Hegathe?" asked the Potentate.

"Morwha?" asked the Emperor. "I've forgotten: which god is that?"

"Lusty fertility goddess of the Yokudans," replied the Potentate. "But not too lusty, like Dibella. Demure, but certainly sexual."

"I am through with lusty women. The Empress, Rijja, all too lusty, a lust for love leads to a lust for power," the Emperor shrugged his shoulders. "But a priestess-in-training with a certain healthy appetite sounds ideal. Now what were you saying about the Black Gate?"

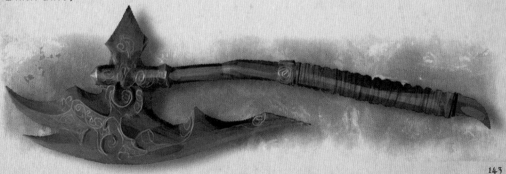

6 Sun's Height, 2920
Thurzo Fortress, Cyrodiil

Rijja stood quietly looking at the cold stone floor while the Emperor spoke. He had never before seen her so pale and joyless. She might at least be pleased that she was being freed, being returned to her homeland. Why, if she left now, she could be in Hammerfell by the Merchant's Festival. Nothing he said seemed to register any reaction from her. A month and a half's stay in Thurzo Fortress seemed to have killed her spirit.

"I was thinking," said the Emperor at last. "Of having your younger sister Corda up to the palace for a time. I think she would prefer it over the conservatorium in Hegathe, don't you?"

Reaction, at last. Rijja looked at the Emperor with animal hatred, flinging herself at him in a rage. Her fingernails had grown long since her imprisonment and she raked them across his face, into his eyes. He howled with pain, and his guards pulled her off, pummeling her with blows from the back of their swords, until she was knocked unconscious.

A healer was called at once, but the Emperor Reman III had lost his right eye.

23 Sun's Height, 2920
Balmora, Morrowind

Vivec pulled himself from the water, feeling the heat of the day washed from his skin, taking a towel from one of his servants. Sotha Sil watched his old friend from the balcony.

"It looks like you've picked up a few more scars since I last saw you," said the sorcerer.

"Azura grant it that I have no more for a while," laughed Vivec. "When did you arrive?"

"A little over an hour ago," said Sotha Sil, walking down the stairs to the water's edge. "I thought I was coming to end a war, but it seems you've done it without me."

"Yes, eighty years is long enough for ceaseless battle," replied Vivec, embracing Sotha Sil. "We made concessions, but so did they. When the old Emperor is dead, we may be entering a golden age. Prince Juilek is very wise for his age. Where is Almalexia?"

"Collecting the Duke of Mournhold. They should be here tomorrow afternoon."

The men were distracted at a sight from around the corner of the palace — a rider was approaching through the town, heading for the front steps. It was evident that the woman had been riding hard for some time. They met her in the study, where she burst in, breathing hard.

"We have been betrayed," she gasped. "The Imperial Army has seized the Black Gate."

24 Sun's Height, 2920
Balmora, Morrowind

It was the first time in seventeen years that the three members of the Morrowind Tribunal had met in the same place, since Sotha Sil had left for Artaeum. All three wished that the circumstances of their reunion were different.

"From what we've learned, while the Prince was returning to Cyrodiil to the south, a second Imperial Army came down from the north," said Vivec to his stony-faced compatriots. "It is reasonable to assume Juilek didn't know about the attack."

"But neither would it be unreasonable to suppose that he planned on being a distraction while the Emperor launched the attack on Black Gate," said Sotha Sil. "This must be considered a break of the truce."

"Where is the Duke of Mournhold?" asked Vivec. "I would hear his thoughts on the matter."

"He is meeting with the Night Mother in Tel Aruhn," said Almalexia, quietly. "I told him to wait until he had spoken with you, but he said that the matter had waited long enough."

"He would involve the Morag Tong? In outside affairs?" Vivec shook his head, and looked to Sotha Sil: "Please, do what you can. Assassination will only move us backwards. This matter must be settled with diplomacy or battle."

25 Sun's Height, 2920
Tel Aruhn, Morrowind

The Night Mother met Sotha Sil in her salon, lit only by the moon. She was cruelly beautiful dressed in a simple silk black robe, lounging across her divan. With a gesture, she dismissed her red-cloaked guards and offered the sorcerer some wine.

"You've only just missed your friend, the Duke," she whispered. "He was very unhappy, but I think we will solve his problem for him."

"Did he hire the Morag Tong to assassinate the Emperor?" asked Sotha Sil.

"You are straight-forward, aren't you? That's good. I love plain-speaking men: it saves so much time. Of course, I cannot discuss with you what the Duke and I talked about," she smiled. "It would be bad for business."

"What if I were to offer you an equal amount of gold for you not to assassinate the Emperor?"

"The Morag Tong murders for the glory of Mephala and for profit," she said, speaking into her glass of wine. "We do not merely kill. That would be sacrilege. Once the Duke's gold has arrived in three days time, we will do our end of the business. And I'm afraid we would not dream of entertaining a counter offer. Though we are a business as well as a religious order, we do not bow to supply and demand, Sotha Sil."

27 Sun's Height, 2920
The Inner Sea, Morrowind

Sotha Sil had been watching the waters for two days now, waiting for a particular vessel, and now he saw it. A heavy ship with the flag of Mournhold. The sorcerer took the air and intercepted it before it reached harbor. A caul of flame erupted over his figure, disguising his voice and form into that of a Daedra.

"Abandon your ship!" he bellowed. "If you would not sink with it!"

In truth, Sotha Sil could have exploded the vessel with but a single ball of fire, but he chose to take his time, to give the crew a chance to dive off into the warm water. When he was certain there was no one living aboard, he focused his energy into a destructive wave that shook the air and water as it discharged. The ship and the Duke's payment to the Morag Tong sunk to the bottom of the Inner Sea.

"Night Mother," thought Sotha Sil, as he floated towards shore to alert the harbormaster that some sailors were in need of rescue. "Everyone bows to supply and demand."

Book Eight: Last Seed

1 Last Seed, 2920
Mournhold, Morrowind

They were gathered in the Duke's courtyard at twilight, enjoying the smell and warmth of a fire of dry branches and bittergreen leaves. Tiny embers flew into the sky, hanging for a few moments before vanishing.

"I was rash," agreed the Duke, soberly. "But Lorkhan had his laugh, and all is well. The Morag Tong will not assassinate the Emperor now that my payment to them is at the bottom of the Inner Sea. I thought you had made some sort of a truce with the Daedra princes."

"What your sailors called a daedra may not have been one," said Sotha Sil. "Perhaps it was a rogue battlemage or even a lightning bolt that destroyed your ship."

"The Prince and the Emperor are en route to take possession of Ald Lambasi as our truce agreed. It is certainly typical of the Cyrodiil to assume that their concessions are negotiable, while ours are not," Vivec pulled out a map. "We can meet them here, in this village to the north-west of Ald Lambasi, Fervinthil."

"But will we meet them to talk," ask Almalexia. "Or to make war?"

No one had an answer to that.

15 Last Seed, 2920

Fervinthil, Morrowind

A late summer squall blew through the small village, darkening the sky except for flashing of lightning which leapt from cloud to cloud like acrobats. Water rushed down the narrow streets ankle-deep, and the Prince had to shout to be heard by his captains but a few feet away from him.

"There's an inn up ahead! We'll wait there for the storm to pass before pressing on to Ald Lambasi!"

The inn was warm and dry, and bustling with business. Barmaids were rushing back and forth, bringing greef and wine to a back room, evidently excited about a famous visitor. Someone who was attracting more attention than the mere heir to the Empire of Tamriel. Amused, Juilek watched them run until he overheard the name of "Vivec."

"My Lord Vivec," he said, bursting into the back room. "You must believe me, I knew nothing about the attack on Black Gate until after it happened. We will, of course, be returning it to your care forthwith. I wrote you a letter to that effect at your palace in Balmora, but obviously you're not there," he paused, taking in the many new faces in the room. "I'm sorry, let me introduce myself. I'm Juilek Cyrodiil."

"My name is Almalexia," said the most beautiful woman the Prince had ever seen. "Won't you join us?"

"Sotha Sil," said a serious-looking Dunmer in a white cloak, shaking the Prince's hand and showing him to a seat.

"Indoril Brindisi Dorom, Duke-Prince of Mournhold," said the massively-built man next to him as he sat down.

"I recognize that the events of the last month suggest, at best, that the Imperial Army is not under my control," said the Prince after ordering some wine. "This is true. The army is my father's."

"I understood that the Emperor was going to be coming to Ald Lambasi as well," said Almalexia.

"Officially, he is," said the Prince cautiously. "Unofficially, he's still back in the Imperial City. He's met with an unfortunate accident."

Vivec glanced the Duke quickly before looking at the Prince: "An accident?"

"He's fine," said the Prince quickly. "He'll live, but it looks like he'll lose an eye. It was an altercation that has nothing to do with the war. The only good news is that while he recovers, I have the use of his seal. Any agreement we make here and now will be binding to the Empire, both in my father's reign and in mine."

"Then let's start agreeing," smiled Almalexia.

16 Last Seed, 2920

Wroth Naga, Cyrodiil

The tiny hamlet of Wroth Naga greeted Cassyr with its colorful houses perched on a promontory overlooking the stretch of the Wrothgarian mountainplain and High Rock beyond. Had he been in a better mood, the sight would have been breathtaking. As it was, he could only think that in practical terms, a small village like this would have meager provisions for himself and his horse.

He rode down into the main square, where an inn called the Eagle's Cry stood. Directing the stable boy to house and feed his horse, Cassyr walked into the inn and was surprised by its ambience. A minstrel he had heard play once in Gilverdale was performing a jaunty old tune to the clapping of the mountain men. Such forced merriment was not what Cassyr wanted at that moment. A glum Dunmer woman was seated at the only table far from the noise, so he took his drink there and sat down without invitation. It was only when he did so that he noticed that she was holding a newborn baby.

"I've just come from Morrowind," he said rather awkwardly, lowering his voice. "I've been fighting for Vivec and the Duke of Mournhold against the Imperial army. A traitor to my people, I guess you'd call me."

"I am also a traitor to my people," said the woman, holding up her hand which was scarred with a branded symbol. "It means that I can never go back to my homeland."

"Well, you're not thinking of staying here, are you?" laughed Cassyr. "It's certainly quaint, but come wintertide, there's going to be snow up to your eyelashes. It's no place for a new baby. What is her name?"

"Bosriel. It means 'Beauty of the Forest.' Where are you going?"

"Dwynnen, on the bay in High Rock. You're welcome to join me, I could use the company." He held out his hand. "Cassyr Whitley."

"Turala," said the woman after a pause. She was going to use her family's name first, as is tradition, but she realized that it was no longer her name. "I would love to accompany you, thank you."

19 Last Seed, 2920

Ald Lambasi, Morrowind

Five men and two women stood in the silence of the Great Room of the castle, the only sound the scrawl of quill on parchment and the gentle tapping of rain on the large picture window. As the Prince set the seal of Cyrodiil on the document, the peace was made official. The Duke of Mournhold broke out in a roar of delight, ordering wine brought in to commemorate the end of eighty years of war.

Only Sotha Sil stood apart from the group. His face betrayed no emotion. Those who knew him best knew he did not believe in endings or beginnings, but in the continuous cycle of which this was but a small part.

"My Prince," said the castle steward, unhappy at breaking the celebration. "There is a messenger here from your mother, the Empress. He asked to see your father, but as he did not arrive —"

Juilek excused himself and went to speak with the messenger.

"The Empress does not live in the Imperial City?" asked Vivec.

"No," said Almalexia, shaking her head sadly. "Her husband has imprisoned her in Black Marsh, fearing that she was plotting a revolution against him. She is extremely wealthy and has powerful allies in the western Colovian estates so he could not marry another or have her executed. They've been at an impasse for the last seventeen years since Juilek was a child."

The Prince returned a few minutes later. His face betrayed his anxiety, though he took troubles to hide it.

"My mother needs me," he said simply. "I'm afraid I must leave at once. If I may have a copy of the treaty, I will bring it with me to show the Empress the good we have done today, and then I will carry it on to the Imperial City so it may be made official."

Prince Juilek left with the fond farewells of the Three of Morrowind. As they watched him ride out into the rainswept night south towards Black Marsh, Vivec said, "Tamriel will be much healed when he has the throne."

1 Last Seed, 2920
Dorsza Pass, Black Marsh

The moon was rising over the desolate quarry, steaming with swamp gas from a particularly hot summer as the Prince and his two guard escort rode out of the forest. The massive piles of earth and dung had been piled high in antiquity by some primitive, long-dead tribe of Black Marsh, hoping to keep out some evil from the north. Evidently, the evil had broken through at Dorsza Pass, the large crack in the sad, lonely rampart that stretched for miles.

The black twisted trees that grew on the barrier cast strange shadows down, like a net tangling. The Prince's mind was on his mother's cryptic letter, hinting at the threat of an invasion. He could not, of course, tell the Dunmer about it, at the very least until he knew more and had notified his father. After all, the letter was meant for him. It was its urgent tone that made him decide to go directly to Gideon.

The Empress had also warned him about a band of former slaves who attacked caravans going into Dorsza Pass. She advised him to be certain to make his Imperial shield visible, so they would know he was not one of the hated Dunmer slavers. Upon riding into the tall weeds that flooded through the pass like a noxious river, the Prince ordered that his shield be displayed.

"I can see why the slaves use this," said the Prince's captain. "It's an excellent location for an ambush."

Juilek nodded his head, but his thoughts were elsewhere. What threat of invasion could the Empress have discovered? Were the Akaviri on the seas again? If so, how could his mother from her cell in Castle Giovese know of it? A rustle in the weeds and a single sharp human cry behind him interrupted his ponderings.

Turning around, the Prince discovered that he was alone. His escort had vanished.

The Prince peered over the stretch of the moonlit sea of grass which waved in almost hypnotic patterns to the ebb and flow of the night wind billowing through the pass. It was impossible to tell if a struggling soldier was beneath this system of vibrations, a dying horse behind another. A high, whistling wind drowned out any sound the victims of the ambush might be making.

Juilek drew his sword, and thought about what to do, his mind willing his heart not to panic. He was closer to the exit of the pass than the entrance. Whatever had slain his escort must have been behind him. If he rode fast enough, perhaps he could outrun it. Spurring his horse to gallop, he charged for the hills ahead, framed by the mighty black piles of dirt.

When he was thrown, it happened so suddenly, he was hurtling forward before he was truly conscious of the fact. He landed several yards beyond where his horse had fallen, breaking his shoulder and his back on impact. A numbness washed over him as he stared at his poor, dying steed, its belly sliced open by one of several spears jutting up just below the surface of the grass.

Prince Juilek was not able to turn and face the figure that emerged from the grass, nor able to move to defend himself. His throat was cut without ceremony. Miramor cursed when he saw the face of his victim more clearly in the moonlight. He had seen the Emperor at the Battle of Bodrum when he had fought in His Imperial Majesty's command, and this was clearly not the Emperor. Searching the body, he found the letter and a treaty signed by Vivec, Almalexia, Sotha Sil, and the Duke of Mournhold representing Morrowind and the Prince Juilek Cyrodiil, representing the Cyrodiil Empire.

"Curse my luck," muttered Miramor to himself and the whispering grass. "I've only killed a Prince. Where's the reward in that?"

Miramor destroyed the letter, as Zuuk had instructed him to do, and pocketed the treaty. At the very least, such a curiosity would have some market value. He disassembled the traps as he pondered his next step. Return to Gideon and ask his employer for a lesser reward for killing the heir? Move on to other lands? At the very least, he considered, he had picked up two useful skills from the Battle of Bodrum. From the Dunmer, he had learned the excellent spear trap. And abandoning the Imperial army, he had learned how to skulk in the grass.

Book Nine: Hearth Fire

2 Hearth Fire, 2920
Gideon, Black Marsh

The Empress Tavia lay across her bed, a hot late summer wind she could not feel banging the shutters of her cell to and fro against the iron bars. Her throat felt like it was on fire but still she sobbed, uncontrollably, wringing her last tapestry in her hands. Her wailing echoed throughout the hollow halls of Castle Giovese, stopping maids in their washing and guards in their conversation. One of her women came up the narrow stairs to see her mistress, but her chief guard Zuuk stood at the doorway and shook his head.

"She's just heard that her son is dead," he said quietly.

5 Hearth Fire, 2920
The Imperial City, Cyrodiil

"Your Imperial Majesty," said the Potentate Versidue-Shaie through the door. "You can open the door. I assure you, you're perfectly safe. No one wants to kill you."

"Mara's blood!" came the Emperor Reman III's voice, muffled, hysterical, tinged with madness. "Someone assassinated the Prince, and he was holding my shield! They could have thought he was me!"

"You're certainly correct, your Imperial Majesty," replied the Potentate, expunging any mocking qualities from his voice while his black-slitted eyes rolled contemptuously. "And we must find and punish the evildoer responsible for your son's death. But we cannot do it without you. You must be brave for your Empire."

There was no reply.

"At the very least, come out and sign the order for Lady Rijja's execution," called the Potentate. "Let us dispose of the one traitor and assassin we know of."

A brief pause, and then the sound of furniture scraping across the floor. Reman opened the door just a crack, but the Potentate could see his angry, fearful face, and the terrible mound of ripped tissue that used to be his right eye. Despite the best healers in the Empire, it was still a ghastly souvenir of the Lady Rijja's work in Thurzo Fortress.

"Hand me the order," the Emperor snarled. "I'll sign it with pleasure."

6 Hearth Fire, 2920
Gideon, Cyrodiil

The strange blue glow of the will o' the wisps, a combination, so she'd be told, of swamp gas and spiritual energy, had always frightened Tavia as she looked out her window. Now it seemed strangely comforting. Beyond the bog lay the city of Gideon. It was funny, she thought, that she had never stepped foot in its streets, though she had watched it every day for seventeen years.

"Can you think of anything I've forgotten?" she asked, turning to look back on the loyal Kothringi Zuuk.

"I know exactly what to do," he said simply. He seemed to smile, but the Empress realized that it was only her own face reflected in his silvery skin. She was smiling, and she didn't even realize it.

"Make certain you aren't followed," she warned. "I don't want my husband to know where my gold's been hiding all these years. And do take your share of it. You've been a good friend."

The Empress Tavia stepped forward and dropped from sight into the mists. Zuuk replaced the bars on the tower window, and threw a blanket over some pillows on her bed. With any luck, they would not discover her body on the lawn until morning, at which time he hoped to be halfway to Morrowind.

9 Hearth Fire, 2920
Phyrgias, High Rock

The strange trees on all sides resembled knobby piles crowned with great bursts of reds, yellows, and oranges, like insect mounds caught fire. The wrothgarian mountains were fading into the misty afternoon. Turala marveled at the sight, so alien, so different from Morrowind, as she plodded the horse forward into an open pasture. Behind her, head nodding against his chest, Cassyr slept, cradling Bosriel. For a moment, Turala considered jumping the low painted fence that crossed the field, but she thought better of it. Let Cassyr sleep for a few more hours before giving him the reigns.

As the horse passed into the field, Turala saw the small green house on the next hill, half-hidden in forest. So picturesque was the image, she felt herself lull into a pleasant half-sleeping state. A blast of a horn brought her back to reality with a shudder. Cassyr opened his eyes.

"Where are we?" he hissed.

"I don't know," Turala stammered, wide-eyed. "What is that sound?"

"Orcs," he whispered. "A hunting party. Head for the thicket quickly."

Turala trotted the horse into the small collection of trees. Cassyr handed her the child and dismounted. He began pulling their bags off next, throwing them into the bushes. A sound started then, a distant rumbling of footfall, growing louder and closer. Turala climbed off carefully and helped Cassyr unburden the horse. All the while, Bosriel watched open-eyed. Turala sometimes worried that her baby never cried. Now she was grateful for it. With the last of the luggage off, Cassyr slapped the horse's rear, sending it galloping into the field. Taking Turala's hand, he hunkered down in the bushes.

"With luck," he murmured. "They'll think she's wild or belongs to the farm and won't go looking for the rider."

As he spoke, a horde of orcs surged into the field, blasting their horns. Turala had seen orcs before, but never in such abundance, never with such bestial confidence. Roaring with delight at the horse and its confused state, they hastened past the timber where Cassyr, Turala, and Bosriel hid. The wildflowers flew into the air at their stampede, powdering the air with seeds. Turala tried to hold back a sneeze, and thought she succeeded. One of the orcs heard something though, and brought another with him to investigate.

Cassyr quietly unsheathed his sword, mustering all the confidence he could. His skills, such as they were, were in spying, not combat, but he vowed to protect Turala and her babe for as long as he could. Perhaps he would slay these two, he reasoned, but not before they cried out and brought the rest of the horde.

Suddenly, something invisible swept through the bushes like a wind. The orcs flew backwards, falling dead on their backs. Turala turned and saw a wrinkled crone with bright red hair emerge from a nearby bush.

"I thought you were going to bring 'em right to me," she whispered, smiling. "Best come with me."

The three followed the old woman through a deep crevasse of bramble bushes that ran through the field toward the house on the hill. As they emerged on the other side, the woman turned to look at the orcs feasting on the remains of the horse, a blood-soaked orgy to the beat of multiple horns.

"That horse yours?" she asked. When Cassyr nodded, she laughed loudly. "That's rich meat, that is. Those monsters'll have bellyaches and flatulence in the morning. Serves 'em right."

"Shouldn't we keep moving?" whispered Turala, unnerved by the woman's laughter.

"They won't come up here," she grinned, looking at Bosriel who smiled back. "They're too afraid of us."

Turala turned to Cassyr, who shook his head. "Witches. Am I correct in assuming that this is Old Barbyn's Farm, the home of the Skeffington Coven?"

"You are, pet," the old woman giggled girlishly, pleased to be so infamous. "I am Mynista Skeffington."

"What did you do to those orcs?" asked Turala. "Back there in the thicket?"

"Spirit fist right side the head," Mynista said, continuing the climb up the hill. Ahead of them was the farmhouse grounds, a well, a chicken coop, a pond, women of all ages doing chores, the laughter of children at play. The old woman turned and saw that Turala did not understand. "Don't you have witches where you come from, child?"

"None that I know of," she said.

"There are all sorts of wielders of magic in Tamriel," she explained. "The Psijics magic like its their painful duty. The battlemages in the army on the other end of the scale hurl spells like arrows. We witches commune and conjure and celebrate. To fell those orcs, I merely whispered to the spirits of the air, Amaro, Pina, Tallatha, the fingers of Kynareth, and the breath of the world, with whom I have an intimate acquaintance, to smack those bastards dead. You see, conjuration is not about might, or solving riddles, or agonizing over musty old scrolls. It's about fostering relations. Being friendly, you might say."

"Well, we certainly appreciate you being friendly with us," said Cassyr.

"As well you might," coughed Mynista. "Your kind destroyed the orc homeland two thousand years ago. Before that, they never came all the way up here and bothered us. Now let's get you cleaned up and fed."

With that, Mynista led them into the farm, and Turala met the family of the Skeffington Coven.

11 Hearth Fire, 2920
The Imperial City, Cyrodiil

Rijja had not even tried to sleep the night before, and she found the somber music played during her execution to have a soporific effect. It was as if she was willing herself to be unconscious before the ax stroke. Her eyes were bound so she could not see her former lover, the Emperor, seated before her, glaring with his one good eye. She could not see the Potentate Versidue-Shaie, his coil neatly wrapped beneath him, a look of triumph in his golden face. She could feel, numbly, the executioner's hand touch her back to steady her. She flinched like a dreamer trying to awake.

The first blow caught the back of her head and she screamed. The next hacked through her neck, and she was dead.

The Emperor turned to the Potentate wearily, "Now that's done. You said she had a pretty sister in Hammerfell named Corda?"

1s Hearth Fire, 2920
Dwynnen, High Rock

The horse the witches had sold him was not as good as his old one, Cassyr considered. Spirit worship and sacrifice and sisterhood might be all well and good for conjuring spirits, but it tends to spoil beasts of burden. Still, there was little to complain about. With the Dunmer woman and her child gone, he had made excellent time. Ahead were the walls surrounding the city of his homeland. Almost at once, he was set upon by his old friends and family.

"How went the war?" cried his cousin, running to the road. "Is it true that Vivec signed a peace with the Prince, but the Emperor refuses to honor it?"

"That's not how it was, was it?" asked a friend, joining them. "I heard that the Dunmer had the Prince murdered and then made up a story about a treaty, but there's no evidence for it."

"Isn't there anything interesting happening here?" Cassyr laughed. "I really don't have the least interest in discussing the war or Vivec."

"You missed the procession of the Lady Corda," said his friend. "She came across the bay with full entourage and then east to the Imperial City."

"But that's nothing. What was Vivec like?" asked his cousin eagerly. "He supposed to be a living god."

"If Sheogorath steps down and they need another God of Madness, he'll do," said Cassyr haughtily.

"And the women?" asked the lad, who had only seen Dunmer ladies on very rare occasions.

Cassyr merely smiled. Turala Skeffington flashed into his mind for an instant before fading away. She would be happy with the coven, and her child would be well cared for. But they were part of the past now, a place and a war he wanted to forget forever. Dismounting his horse, he walked it into the city, chatting of trivial gossip of life on the Iliac Bay.

Book Ten: Frostfall

10 Frostfall, 2920
Phrygias, High Rock

The creature before them blinked, senseless, its eyes glazed, mouth opening and closing as if relearning its function. A thin glob of saliva burbled down, hanging suspended between its fangs. Turala had never seen anything of its kind before, reptilian and massive, perched on its hind legs like a man. Mynistera applauded enthusiastically.

"My child," she crowed. "You have come so far in so short a time. What were you thinking when you summoned this daedroth?"

It took Turala a moment to recall whether she was thinking anything at all. She was merely overwhelmed that she had reached out across the fabric of reality into the realm of Oblivion, and plucked forth this loathsome creature, conjuring it into the world by the power of her mind.

"I was thinking of the color red," Turala said, concentrating. "The simplicity and clarity of it. And then — I desired, and spoke the charm. And this is what I conjured up."

"Desire is a powerful force for a young witch," said Mynistera. "And it is well matched in this instance. For this daedroth is nothing if not a simple force of the spirits. Can you release your desire as easily?"

Turala closed her eyes and spoke the dismissal invocation. The monster faded away like a painting in sunlight, still blinking confusedly. Mynistera embraced her Dark Elf pupil, laughing with delight.

"I never would have believed it, a month and a day you've been with the coven, and you're already far more advanced than most of the women here. There is powerful blood in you, Turala, you touch spirits like you were touching a lover. You'll be leading this coven one day — I have seen it!"

Turala smiled. It was good to be complimented. The Duke of Mournhold had praised her pretty face; and her family, before she had dishonored them, praised her manners. Cassyr had been nothing more than a companion: his compliments meant nothing. But with Mynistera, she felt she was home.

"You'll be leading the coven for many years yet, great sister," said Turala.

"I certainly intend to. But the spirits, while marvelous companions and faultless tellers of truth, are often hazy about the when and hows. You can't blame them really. When and how mean so little to them," Mynistera opened the door to the shed, allowing the brisk autumn breeze in to dispel the bitter and fetid smells of the daedroth. "Now, I need you to run an errand to Wayrest. It's only a week's ride there, and a week's ride back. Bring Doryatha and Celephyna with you. As much as we try to be self-sufficient, there are herbs we can't grow here, and we seem to run through an enormous quantity of gems in no time at all. It's important that the people of the city learn to recognize you as one of the wise women of Skeffington coven. You'll find the benefits of being notorious far outweigh the inconveniences."

Turala did as she was bade. As she and her sisters climbed aboard their horses, Mynistera brought her child, little five-month-old Bosriel to kiss her mother good-bye. The witches were in love with the little Dunmer infant, fathered by a wicked Duke, birthed by wild Ayleid elves in the forest heart of the Empire. Turala knew her nursemaids would protect her child with their lives. After many kisses and a farewell wave, the three young witches rode off into the bright woods, under a covering of red, yellow, and orange.

12 Frostfall, 2920
Dwynnen, High Rock

For a Middas evening, the Least Loved Porcupine tavern was wildly crowded. A roaring fire in the pit in the center of the room cast an almost sinister glow on all the regulars, and made the abundance of bodies look like a punishment tapestry inspired by the Arcturian Heresies. Cassyr took his usual place with his cousin and ordered a flagon of ale.

"Have you been to see the Baron?" asked Palyth.

"Yes, he may have work for me in the palace of Urvaius," said Cassyr proudly. "But more than that I can't say. You understand, secrets of state and all that. Why are there so many damned people here tonight?"

"A shipload of Dark Elves just came in to harbor. They've come from the war. I was just waiting until you got here to introduce you as another veteran."

Cassyr blushed, but regained his composure enough to ask: "What are they doing here? Has there been a truce?"

"I don't know the full story," said Palyth. "But apparently, the Emperor and Vivec are in negotiations again. These fellas here have investments they were keen to check on, and they figured things on the Bay were quiet enough. But the only way we can get the full story is to talk to the chaps."

With that, Palyth gripped his cousin's arm and pulled him to the other side of the bar so suddenly, Cassyr would have had to struggle violently to resist. The Dunmer travelers were spread out across four of the tables, laughing with the locals. They were largely amiable young men, well-dressed, befitting merchants, animated in gesture made more extravagant by liquor.

"Excuse me," said Palyth, intruding on the conversation. "My shy cousin Cassyr was in the war as well, fighting for the living god, Vivec."

"The only Cassyr I ever heard of," said one of the Dunmer drunkenly with a wide, friendly smile, shaking Cassyr's free hand. "Was a Cassyr Whitley, who Vivec said was the worst spy in history. We lost Ald Marak due to his bungling intelligence work. For your sake, friend, I hope the two of you were never confused."

Cassyr smiled and listened as the lout told the story of his failure with bountiful exaggerations which caused the table to roar with laughter. Several eyes looked his way, but none of the locals sought to explain that the fool of the tale was standing at attention. The eyes that stung the most were his cousin's, the young man who had believed that he had returned to Dwynnen a great hero. At some point, certainly, the Baron would hear about it, his idiocy increasing manifold with each retelling.

With every fiber in his soul, Cassyr cursed the living god Vivec.

21 Frostfall, 2920
The Imperial City, Cyrodiil

Corda, in a robe of blinding whiteness, a uniform of the priestesses of the Hegathe Morwha conservatorium, arrived in the City just as the first winter storm was passing. The clouds broke with sunlight, and the beauteous teenaged Redguard girl appeared in the wide avenue with escort, riding toward the Palace. While her sister was tall, thin, angular, and haughty, Corda was a small, round-faced lass with wide brown eyes. The locals were quick to draw comparisons.

"Not a month after Lady Rijja's execution," muttered a housemaid, peering out the window, and winking to her neighbor.

"And not a month out of the nunnery neither," the other woman agreed, reveling in the scandal. "This one's in for a ride. Her sister weren't no innocent, and look where she ended up."

24 Frostfall, 2920
Dwynnen, High Rock

Cassyr stood on the harbor and watched the early sleet fall on the water. It was a pity, he thought, that he was prone to sea-sickness. There was nothing for him now in Tamriel to the east or to the west. Vivec's tale of his poor spycraft had spread to taverns everywhere. The Baron of Dwynnenhad released him from his contract. No doubt they were laughing about him in Daggerfall, too, and Dawnstar, Lilmoth, Rimmen, Greenheart, probably in Akavir and Yokuda for that matter. Perhaps it would be best to drop into the waves and sink. The thought, however, did not stay long in his mind: it was not despair that haunted him, but rage. Impotent fury that he could not assuage.

"Excuse me, sir," said a voice behind him, making him jump. "I'm sorry to disturb you, but I was wondering whether you could recommend an inexpensive tavern for me to spend the night."

It was a young man, a Nord, with a sack over his shoulder. Obviously, he had just disembarked from one of the boats. For the first time in weeks, someone was looking at Cassyr as something other than a colossal, famous idiot. He could not help, black as his mood was, but be friendly.

"You've just arrived from Skyrim?" asked Cassyr.

"No, sir, that's where I'm going," said the fellow. "I'm working my way home. I've come up from Sentinel, and before that Stros M'kai, and before that Woodhearth in Valenwood, and before that Artaeum in Summurset. Welleg's my name."

Cassyr introduced himself and shook Welleg's hand. "Did you say you came from Artaeum? Are you a Psijic?"

"No, sir, not anymore," the fellow shrugged. "I was expelled."

"Do you know anything about summoning daedra? You see, I want to cast a curse against a particularly powerful person, one might say a living god, and I haven't had any luck. The Baron won't allow me in his sight, but the Baroness has sympathy for me and allowed me the use of their Summoning Chambers." Cassyr spat. "I did all the rituals, made sacrifices, but nothing came of it."

"That'd be because of Sotha Sil, my old master," replied Welleg with some bitterness. "The Daedra princes have agreed not to be summoned by any amateurs at least until the war ends. Only the Psijics may counsel with the daedra, and a few nomadic sorcerers and witches."

"Witches, did you say?"

29 Frostfall, 2920
Phrygias, High Rock

Pale sunlight flickered behind the mist bathing the forest as Turala, Doryatha, and Celephyna drove their horses on. The ground was wet with a thin layer of frost, and laden down with goods, it was a slippery way over unpaved hills. Turala tried to contain her excitement about coming back to the coven. Wayrest had been an adventure, and she adored the looks of fear and respect the cityfolk gave her. But for the last few days, all she could think of was returning to her sisters and her child.

A bitter wind whipped her hair forward so she could see nothing but the path ahead. She did not hear the rider approach to her side until he was almost upon her. When she turned and saw Cassyr, she shouted with as much surprise as pleasure at meeting an old friend. His face was pale and drawn, but she took it to be merely from travel.

"What brings you back to Phrygias?" she smiled. "Were you not treated well in Dwynnen?"

"Well enough," said Cassyr. "I have need of the Skeffington coven."

"Ride with us," said Turala. "I'll bring you to Mynistera."

The four continued on, and the witches regaled Cassyr with tales of Wayrest. It was evident that it was also a rare treat for Doryatha and Celephyna to leave Old Barbyn's Farm. They had been born there, as daughters and grand-daughters of Skeffington witches. Ordinary High Rock city life was exotic to them as it was to Turala. Cassyr said little, but smiled and nodded his head, which was encouragement enough. Thankfully, none of the stories they had heard were about his own stupidity. Or at the very least, they did not tell him.

Doryatha was in the midst of a tale she had heard in a tavern about a thief who had been locked overnight in a pawnshop when they crossed over a familiar hill. Suddenly, she halted in her story. The barn was supposed to be visible, but it was not. The other three followed her gaze into the fog, and a moment later, they rode as fast as they could towards what was once the site of the Skeffington coven.

The fire had long since burned out. Nothing but ashes, skeletons, and broken weaponry remained. Cassyr recognized at once the signs of an orc raid.

The witches fell from their horses, racing through the remains, wailing. Celephyna found a tattered, bloody piece of cloth that she recognized from Mynistera's cloak. She held it to her ashen face, sobbing. Turala screamed for Bosriel, but the only reply was the high whistling wind through the ashes.

"Who did this?" she cried, tears streaking down her face. "I swear I'll conjure up the very flames of Oblivion! What have they done with my baby?"

"I know who did it," said Cassyr quietly, dropping from his horse and walking towards her. "I've seen these weapons before. I fear I met the very fiends responsible in Dwynnen, but I never thought they'd find you. This is the work of assassins hired by the Duke of Mournhold."

He paused. The lie came easily. Adopt and improvise. What's more, he could tell instantly that she believed it. Her resentment over the cruelty the Duke had shown her had quieted, but never disappeared. One look at her burning eyes told him that she would summon the daedra and wreak his, and her, revenge upon Morrowind. And what's more, he knew they'd listen.

And listen they did. For the power that is greater than desire is rage. Even rage misplaced.

Book Eleven: Sun's Dusk

2 Sun's Dusk, 2920
Tel Aruhn, Morrowind

man to see you, Night Mother," said the guard. "A Kothringi tribesman who presents his credentials as Lord Zuuk of Black Marsh, part of the Imperial Garrison of Gideon."

"What makes you think I'd have even the slightest possible interest in seeing him?" asked the Night Mother with venomous sweetness.

"He brings a letter from the late Empress of the Cyrodilic Empire."

"We are having a busy day," she smiled, clapping her hands together with delight. "Show him in."

Zuuk entered the chamber. His metallic skin, though exposed only at his face and hands, caught the light of the fireplace and the lightning of the stormy night from the window. The Night Mother noted also that she could see herself as he saw her: serene, beautiful, fear-inspiring. He handed her his letter from the Empress without a word. Sipping her wine, she read it.

"The Duke of Morrowind also offered me an appreciable sum to have the Emperor murdered earlier this year," she said, folding the letter. "His payment sunk, and never was delivered. It was a considerable annoyance, particularly as I had already gone to the trouble of putting one of my agents in the palace. Why should I assume that your more-than-generous payment, from a dead woman, will arrive?"

"I brought it with me," said Zuuk simply. "It is in the carriage outside."

"Then bring it in and our business is complete," smiled the Night Mother. "The Emperor will be dead by year's end. You may leave the gold with Apaladith. Unless you'd care for some wine?"

Zuuk declined the offer and withdrew. The moment he left the room, Miramor slipped noiselessly back from behind the dark tapestry. The Night Mother offered him a glass of wine, and he accepted it.

"I know that fellow, Zuuk," said Miramor carefully. "I didn't know he worked for the old Empress though."

"Let's talk about you some more, if you don't mind," she said, knowing he would, in fact, not mind.

"Let me show you my worth," said Miramor. "Let me be the one to do the Emperor in. I've already killed his son, and you saw there how well I can hide myself away. Tell me you saw one ripple in the tapestry."

The Night Mother smiled. Things were falling into place rather nicely.

"If you know how to use a dagger, you will find him at Bodrum," she said, and described to him what he must do.

3 Sun's Dusk, 2920
Mournhold, Morrowind

The Duke stared out the window. It was early morning, and for the fourth straight day, a red mist hung over the city, flashing lightning. A freakish wind blew through the streets, ripping his flags from the castle battlements, forcing all his people to close their shutters tightly. Something terrible was coming to his land. He was not a greatly learned man, but he knew the signs. So too did his subjects.

"When will my messengers reach the Three?" he growled, turning to his castellan.

"Vivec is far to the north, negotiating the treaty with the Emperor," the man said, his face and voice trembling with fear. "Almalexia and Sotha Sil are in Necrom. Perhaps they can be reached in a few days time."

The Duke nodded. He knew his messengers were fast, but so too was the hand of Oblivion.

6 Sun's Dusk, 2920
Bodrum, Morrowind

Torchlight caught in the misting snow gave the place an otherworldly quality. The soldiers from both camps found themselves huddled together around the largest of the bonfires: winter bringing enemies of four score years of warring close together. While only a few of the Dunmer guard could speak Cyrodilic, they found common ground battling for warmth. When a pretty Redguard maiden passed into their midst to warm herself before moving back to the treaty tent, many a man from both armies raised their eyes in approval.

The Emperor Reman III was eager to leave negotiations before they had ever begun. A month earlier, he thought it would be a sign of good will to meet at the site of his defeat to Vivec's army, but the place brought back more bad memories than he thought it would. Despite the protestations of Potentate Versidue-Shaie that the rocks of the river were naturally red, he could swear he saw splatters of his soldier's blood.

"We have all the particulars of the treaty," he said, taking a glass of hot yuelle from his mistress Corda. "But here and now is not the place for signing. We should do it at the Imperial Palace, with all the pomp and splendor this historic occasion demands. You must bring Almalexia with you also; and that wizard fellow."

"Sotha Sil," whispered the Potentate.

"When?" asked Vivec with infinite patience.

"In exactly a month's time," said the Emperor, smiling munificently and clambering awkwardly to his feet. "We will hold a grand ball to commemorate. Now I must take a walk. My legs are all cramped up with the weather. Corda, my dear, will you walk with me?"

"Of course, your Imperial Majesty," she said, helping him toward the tent's entrance.

"Would you like me to come with you as well, your Imperial Majesty?" asked Versidue-Shaie.

"Or I?" asked King Dro'Zel of Senchal, a newly appointed advisor to the court.

"That won't be necessary, I won't be gone a minute," said Reman.

Miramor crouched in the same rushes he had hidden in nearly eight months before. Now the ground was hard and snow-covered, and the rushes slick with ice. Every slight movement he made issued forth a crunch. If it were not for the raucous songs of the combined Morrowind and Imperial army gathered about the bonfire, he would not have dared creep this close to the Emperor and his concubine. They were standing at the curve in the frozen creek below the bluff, surrounded by trees sparkling with ice.

Carefully, Miramor removed the dagger from its sheath. He had slightly exaggerated his abilities with a short blade to the Night Mother. True, he had used one to cut the throat of Prince Juilek, but the lad was not in any position to fight back at the time. Still, how difficult could it be to stab an old man with one eye? What sort of blade skill would such an easy assassination require?

His ideal moment presented itself before his eyes. The woman saw something deeper in the woods, an icicle of an unusual shape she said, and darted off to get it. The Emperor remained behind, laughing. He turned to the face of the bluff to see his soldiers singing their song's refrain, his back to his assassin. Miramor knew the moment had come. Mindful of the sound of his footfall on the icy ground, he stepped forward and struck. Very nearly.

Almost simultaneously, he was aware of a strong arm holding back his striking arm and another one punching a dagger into his throat. He could not scream. The Emperor, still looking up at the soldiers, never saw Miramor pulled back into the brush and a hand much more skilled than his slicing into his back, paralyzing him.

His blood pooling out and already crystallizing on the frozen ground, Miramor watched, dying, as the Emperor and his courtesan returned to join the camp up on the bluff.

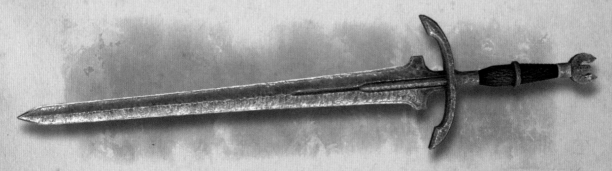

12 Sun's Dusk, 2920
Mournhold, Morrowind

A gout of ever-erupting flame was all that remained of the central courtyard of Castle Mournhold, blasting skyward into the boiling clouds. A thick, tarry smoke rolled through the streets, igniting everything that was wood or paper on fire. Winged bat-like creatures harried the citizens from their hiding places out into the open, where they were met by the real army. The only thing that kept all of Mournhold from burning to the ground was the wet, sputtering blood of its people.

Mehrunes Dagon smiled as he surveyed the castle crumbling.

"To think I nearly didn't come," he said aloud, his voice booming over the chaos. "Imagine missing all this fun."

His attention was arrested by a needle-thin shaft of light piercing through his black and red shadowed sky. He followed it to its source, two figures, a man and a woman standing on the hill above town. The man in the white robe he recognized immediately as Sotha Sil, the sorcerer who had talked all the Princes of Oblivion into that meaningless truce.

"If you've come for the Duke of Mournhold, he isn't here," laughed Mehrunes Dagon. "But you might find pieces of him the next time it rains."

"Daedra, we cannot kill you," said Almalexia, her face hard and resolute. "But that you will soon regret."

With that, two living gods and a prince of Oblivion engaged in battle on the ruins of Mournhold.

17 Sun's Dusk, 2920
Tel Aruhn, Morrowind

"Night Mother," said the guard. "Correspondence from your agent in the Imperial Palace."

The Night Mother read the note carefully. The test had been a success: Miramor had been successfully detected and slain. The Emperor was in very unsafe hands. The Night Mother responded immediately.

18 Sun's Dusk, 2920
Balmora, Morrowind

Sotha Sil, face solemn and unreadable, greeted Vivec at the grand plaza in front of his palace. Vivec had ridden day and night after hearing about the battle in his tent in Bodrum, crossing mile after mile, cutting through the dangerous ground at Dagoth-Ur at blinding speed. To the south, during all the course of the journey, he could see the whirling red clouds and knew that the battle was continuing, day after day. In Gnisis, he met a messenger from Sotha Sil, asking him to meet at Balmora.

"Where is Almalexia?"

"Inside," said Sotha Sil wearily. There was a long, ugly gash running across his jaw. "She's gravely injured, but Mehrunes Dagon will not return from Oblivion for many a moon."

Almalexia lay on a bed of silk, tended to by Vivec's own healers. Her face, even her lips, was gray as stone, and blood stained through the gauze of her bandages. Vivec took her cold hand. Almalexia's mouth moved wordlessly. She was dreaming.

She was battling Mehrunes Dagon again amid a firestorm. All around her, the blackened husk of a castle crumbled, splashing sparks into the night sky. The Daedra's claws dug into her belly, spreading poison through her veins while Almalexia throttled him. As she sank to the ground beside her defeated foe, she saw that the castle consumed by fire was not Castle Mournhold. It was the Imperial Palace.

24 Sun's Dusk, 2920
The Imperial City, Cyrodiil

A winter gale blew over the city, splashing the windows and glass domes of the Imperial Palace. Quivering light rays illuminated the figures within in surreal patterns.

The Emperor barked orders to his staff in preparations for the banquet and ball. This was what he enjoyed best, more than battle. King Dro'Zel was supervising the entertainment, having strong opinions on the matter. The Emperor himself was arranging the details of the dinner. Roast nebfish, vegetable marrow, cream soups, buttered helerac, codscrumb, tongue in aspic. Potentate Versidue-Shaie had made a few suggestions of his own, but the tastes of the Akaviri were very peculiar.

The Lady Corda accompanied the Emperor to his chambers as night fell.

Book Twelve: Evening Star

1 Sun's Dusk, 2920
Balmora, Morrowind

The winter morning sun glinted through the cobweb of frost on the window, and Almalexia opened her eyes. An ancient healer mopped a wet cloth across her head, smiling with relief. Asleep in the chair next to her bed was Vivec. The healer rushed to a side cabinet and returned with a flagon of water.

"How are you feeling, goddess?" asked the healer.

"Like I've been asleep for a very long time," said Almalexia.

"So you have. Fifteen days," said the healer, and touched Vivec's arm. "Master, wake up. She speaks."

Vivec rose with a start, and seeing Almalexia alive and awake, his face broke into a wide grin. He kissed her forehead, and took her hand. At last, there was warmth again in her flesh.

Almalexia's peaceful repose suddenly snapped: "Sotha Sil —"

"He's alive and well," replied Vivec. "Working on one of his machines again somewhere. He would have stayed here too, but he realized he could do you more good working that peculiar sorcery of his."

The castellan appeared in the doorway. "Sorry to interrupt you, master, but I wanted to tell you that your fastest messenger left late last night for the Imperial City."

"Messenger?" asked Almalexia. "Vivec, what has happened?"

"I was to go and sign a truce with the Emperor on the sixth, so I sent him word that it had to be postponed."

"You can't do me any good here," said Almalexia, pulling herself up with effort. "But if you don't sign that truce, you'll put Morrowind back to war, maybe for another eighty years. If you leave today with an escort and hurry, perhaps you can get to the Imperial City only a day or two late."

"Are you certain you don't need me here?" asked Vivec.

"I know that Morrowind needs you more."

6 Sun's Dusk, 2920
The Imperial City, Cyrodiil

The Emperor Reman III sat on his throne, surveying the audience chamber. It was a spectacular sight: silver ribbons dangled from the rafters, burning cauldrons of sweet herbs simmered in every corner, Pyandonean swallowtails sweeping through the air, singing their songs. When the torches were lit and servants began fanning, the room would be transfigured into a shimmering fantasy land. He could smell the kitchen already, spices and roasts.

The Potentate Versidue-Shaie and his son Savirien-Chorak slithered into the room, both bedecked in the headdress and jewelry of the Tsaesci. There was no smile on their golden face, but there seldom was one. The Emperor still greeted his trusted advisor with enthusiasm.

"This ought to impress those savage Dark Elves," he laughed. "When are they supposed to arrive?"

"A messenger's just arrived from Vivec," said the Potentate solemnly. "I think it would be best if your Imperial Majesty met him alone."

The Emperor lost his laughter, but nodded to his servants to withdraw. The door then opened and the Lady Corda walked into the room, with a parchment in her hand. She shut the door behind her, but did not look up to meet the Emperor's face.

"The messenger gave his letter to my mistress?" said Reman, incredulous, rising to take the note. "That's a highly unorthodox way of delivering a message."

"But the message itself is very orthodox," said Corda, looking up into his one good eye. With a single blinding motion, she brought the letter up under the Emperor's chin. His eyes widened and blood poured down the blank parchment. Blank that is, except for a small black mark, the sign of theMorag Tong. It fell to the floor, revealing the small dagger hidden behind it, which she now twisted, severing his throat to the bone. The Emperor collapsed to the floor, gasping soundlessly.

"How long do you need?" asked Savirien-Chorak.

"Five minutes," said Corda, wiping the blood from her hands. "If you can give me ten, though, I'll be doubly grateful."

"Very well," said the Potentate to Corda's back as she raced from the audience chamber. "She ought to have been an Akaviri, the way the girl handles a blade is truly remarkable."

"I must go and establish our alibi," said Savirien-Chorak, disappearing behind one of the secret passages that only the Emperor's most trusted knew about.

"Do you remember, close to a year ago, your Imperial Majesty," the Potentate smiled, looking down at the dying man. "When you told me to remember 'You Akaviri have a lot of showy moves, but if just one of our strikes comes through, it's all over for you.' I remembered that, you see."

The Emperor spat up blood and somehow said the word: "Snake."

"I am a snake, your Imperial Majesty, inside and out. But I didn't lie. There was a messenger from Vivec. It seems he'll be a little late in arriving," the Potentate shrugged before disappearing behind the secret passage. "Don't worry yourself. I'm sure the food won't go bad."

The Emperor of Tamriel died in a pool of his own blood in his empty audience chamber decorated for a grand ball. He was found by his bodyguard fifteen minutes later. Corda was nowhere to be found.

Caer Suvio, Cyrodiil

Lord Gla, apologizing profusely for the quality of the road through the forest, was the first emissary to greet Vivec and his escort as they arrived. A string of burning globes decorated the leafless trees surrounding the villa, bobbing in the gentle but frigid night breeze. From within, Vivec could smell the simple feast and a high sad melody. It was a traditional Akaviri wintertide carol.

Potentate Versidue-Shaie greeted Vivec at the front door.

"I'm glad you received the message before you got all the way to the City," said the Potentate, guiding his guest into the large, warm drawing room. "We are in a difficult transition time, and for the moment, it is best not to conduct our business at the capitol."

"There is no heir?" asked Vivec.

"No official one, though there are distant cousins vying for the throne. While we sort the matter out, at least temporarily the nobles have decided that I may act in the office of my late master," Versidue-Shaie signaled for the servants to draw two comfortable chairs in front of the fireplace. "Would you feel most comfortable if we signed the treaty officially right now, or would you like to eat something first?"

"You intend to honor the Emperor's treaty?"

"I intend to do everything as the Emperor," said the Potentate.

Tel Aruhn, Morrowind

Corda, dusty from the road, flew into the Night Mother's arms. For a moment, they stayed locked together, the Night Mother stroking her daughter's hair, kissing her forehead. Finally, she reached into her sleeve and handed Corda a letter.

"What is it?" asked Corda.

"A letter from the Potentate, expressing his delight at your expertise," replied the Night Mother. "He's promised to send us payment, but I've already sent him back a reply. The late Empress paid us enough for her husband's death. Mephala would not have us be greedy beyond our needs. You should not be paid twice for the same murder, so it is written."

"He killed Rijja, my sister," said Corda quietly.

"And so it should be that you struck the blow."

"Where will I go now?"

"Whenever any of our holy workers becomes too famous to continue the crusade, we send them to an island called Vounoura. It's not more than a month's voyage by boat, and I've arranged for a delightful estate for your sanctuary," the Night Mother kissed the girl's tears. "You meet many friends there, and I know you will find peace and happiness at last, my child."

19 Sun's Dusk, 2920
Mournhold, Morrowind

Almalexia surveyed the rebuilding of the town. The spirit of the citizens was truly inspirational, she thought, as she walked among the skeletons of new buildings standing in the blackened, shattered remains of the old. Even the plant life showed a remarkable resilience. There was life yet in the blasted remains of the comberry and roobrush shrubs that once lined the main avenue. She could feel the pulse. Come springtide, green would bolt through the black.

The Duke's heir, a lad of considerable intelligence and sturdy Dunmer courage, was coming down from the north to take his father's place. The land would do more than survive: it would strengthen and expand. She felt the future much more strongly than she saw the present.

Of all the things she was most certain of, she knew that Mournhold was forever home to at least one goddess.

22 Sun's Dusk, 2920
The Imperial City, Cyrodiil

"The Cyrodiil line is dead," announced the Potentate to the crowd gathered beneath the Speaker's Balcony of the Imperial Palace. "But the Empire lives. The distant relatives of our beloved Emperor have been judged unworthy of the throne by the trusted nobility who advised his Imperial Majesty throughout his long and illustrious reign. It has been decided that as an impartial and faithful friend of Reman III, I will have the responsibility of continuing on in his name."

The Akaviri paused, allowing his words to echo and translate into the ears of the populace. They merely stared up at him in silence. The rain had washed through the streets of the city, but the sun, for a brief time, appeared to be offering a respite from the winter storms.

"I want to make it clear that I am not taking the title Emperor," he continued. "I have been and will continue to be Potentate Versidue-Shaie, an alien welcomed kindly to your shores. It will be my duty to protect my adopted homeland, and I pledge to work tirelessly at this task until someone more worthy takes the burden from me. As my first act, I declare that in commemoration of this historical moment, beginning on the first of Morning Star, we will enter year one of the Second Era as time will be reckoned. Thus, we mourn the loss of our Imperial family, and look forward to the future."

Only one man clapped at these words. King Dro'Zel of Senchal truly believed that this would be the finest thing to happen to Tamriel in history. Of course, he was quite mad.

31 Sun's Dusk, 2920
Ebonheart, Morrowind

In the smoky catacombs beneath the city where Sotha Sil forged the future with his arcane clockwork apparatus, something unforeseen happened. An oily bubble seeped from a long trusted gear and popped. Immediately, the wizard's attention was drawn to it and to the chain that tiny action triggered. A pipe shifted half an inch to the left. A tread skipped. A coil rewound itself and began spinning in a counter direction. A piston that had been thrusting left–right, left–right, for millennia suddenly began shifting right–left. Nothing broke, but everything changed.

"It cannot be fixed now," said the sorcerer quietly.

He looked up through a crick in the ceiling into the night sky. It was midnight.

The second era, the age of chaos, had begun.

Aedra and Daedra

The designations of Gods, Demons, Aedra, and Daedra, are universally confusing to the layman. They are often used interchangeably.

"Aedra" and "Daedra" are not relative terms. They are Elvish and exact. Azura is a Daedra both in Skyrim and Morrowind. "Aedra" is usually translated as "ancestor," which is as close as Cyrodilic can come to this Elven concept. "Daedra" means, roughly, "not our ancestors." This distinction was crucial to the Dunmer, whose fundamental split in ideology is represented in their mythical genealogy.

Aedra are associated with stasis. Daedra represent change.

Aedra created the mortal world and are bound to the Earth Bones. Daedra, who cannot create, have the power to change.

As part of the divine contract of creation, the Aedra can be killed. Witness Lorkhan and the moons.

The protean Daedra, for whom the rules do not apply, can only be banished.

The Book of Daedra

Azura, whose sphere is dusk and dawn, the magic in-between realms of twilight, known as Moonshadow, Mother of the Rose, and Queen of the Night Sky.

Boethiah, whose sphere is deceit and conspiracy, and the secret plots of murder, assassination, treason, and unlawful overthrow of authority.

Clavicus Vile, whose sphere is the granting of power and wishes through ritual invocations and pact.

Hermaeus Mora, whose sphere is scrying of the tides of Fate, of the past and future as read in the stars and heavens, and in whose dominion are the treasures of knowledge and memory.

Hircine, whose sphere is the Hunt, the Sport of Daedra, the Great Game, the Chase, known as the Huntsman and the Father of Manbeasts.

Malacath, whose sphere is the patronage of the spurned and ostracized, the keeper of the Sworn Oath, and the Bloody Curse.

Mehrunes Dagon, whose sphere is Destruction, Change, Revolution, Energy, and Ambition.

Mephala, whose sphere is obscured to mortals; known by the names Webspinner, Spinner, and Spider; whose only consistent theme seems to be interference in the affairs of mortals for her amusement.

Meridia, whose sphere is obscured to mortals; who is associated with the energies of living things.

Molag Bal, whose sphere is the domination and enslavement of mortals; whose desire is to harvest the souls of mortals and to bring mortal souls within his sway by spreading seeds of strife and discord in the mortal realms.

Namira, whose sphere is the ancient Darkness; known as the Spirit Daedra, ruler of sundry dark and shadowy spirits; associated with spiders, insects, slugs, and other repulsive creatures which inspire mortals with an instinctive revulsion.

Nocturnal, whose sphere is the night and darkness; who is known as the Night Mistress.

Peryite, whose sphere is the ordering of the lowest orders of Oblivion, known as the Taskmaster.

Sanguine, whose sphere is hedonistic revelry and debauchery, and passionate indulgences of darker natures.

Sheogorath, whose sphere is Madness, and whose motives are unknowable.

Vaermina, whose sphere is the realm of dreams and nightmares, and from whose realm issues forth evil omens.

Especially marked for special interest under the heading "Malacath" you find a reference to SCOURGE, blessed by Malacath, and dedicated to the use of mortals. In short, the reference suggests that any Daedra attempting to invoke the weapon's powers will be expelled into the voidstreams of Oblivion.

"Of the legendary artifacts of the Daedra, many are well known, like Azura's Star, and Sheogorath's Wabbajack. Others are less well known, like Scourge, Mackkan's Hammer, Bane of Daedra...."

"...yet though Malacath blessed Scourge to be potent against his Daedra kin, he thought not that it should fall into Daedric hands, then to serve as a tool for private war among caitiff and forsaken. Thus did Malacath curse the device such that, should any dark kin seek to invoke its powers, that a void should open and swallow that Daedra, and purge him into Oblivion's voidstreams, from thence to pathfind back to the Real and Unreal Worlds in the full order of time."

Darkest Darkness

Anonymous

In Morrowind, both worshippers and sorcerers summon lesser Daedra and bound Daedra as servants and instruments.

Most Daedric servants can be summoned by sorcerers only for very brief periods, within the most fragile and tenuous frameworks of command and binding. This fortunately limits their capacity for mischief, though in only a few minutes, most of these servants can do terrible harm to their summoners as well as their enemies.

Worshippers may bind other Daedric servants to this plane through rituals and pacts. Such arrangements result in the Daedric servant remaining on this plane indefinitely — or at least until their bodily manifestations on this plane are destroyed, precipitating their supernatural essences back to Oblivion. Whenever Daedra are encountered at Daedric ruins or in tombs, they are almost invariably long-term visitors to our plane.

Likewise, lesser entities bound by their Daedra Lords into weapons and armor may be summoned for brief periods, or may persist indefinitely, so long as they are not destroyed and banished. The class of bound weapons and bound armors summoned by Temple followers and conjurors are examples of short-term bindings; Daedric artifacts like Mehrunes Razor and the Mask of Clavicus Vile are examples of long-term bindings.

The Tribunal Temple of Morrowind has incorporated the veneration of Daedra as lesser spirits subservient to the immortal Almsivi, the Triune godhead of Almalexia, Sotha Sil, and Vivec. These subordinate Daedra are divided into the Good Daedra and the Bad Daedra. The Good Daedra have willingly submitted to the authority of Almsivi; the Bad Daedra are rebels who defy Almsivi — treacherous kin who are more often adversaries than allies.

The Good Daedra are Boethiah, Azura, and Mephala. The hunger is a powerful and violent lesser Daedra associated with Boethiah, Father of Plots — a sinuous, long-limbed, long-tailed creature with a beast-skulled head, noted for its paralyzing touch and its ability to disintegrate weapons and armor. The winged twilight is a messenger of Azura, Goddess of Dusk and Dawn. Winged twilights resemble the feral harpies of the West, though the feminine aspects of the winged twilights are more ravishing, and their long, sharp, hooked tails are immeasurably more deadly. Spider Daedra are the servants of Mephala, taking the form of spider-humanoid centaurs, with a naked upper head, torso, and arms of human proportions, mounted on the eight legs and armored carapace of a giant spider. Unfortunately, these Daedra are so fierce and irrational that they cannot be trusted to heed the commands of the Spinner. As a consequence, few sorcerers are willing to either summon or bind such creatures in Morrowind.

The Bad Daedra are Mehrunes Dagon, Malacath, Sheogorath, and Molag Bal. Three lesser Daedra are associated with Mehrunes Dagon: the agile and pesky scamp, the ferocious and beast-like clannfear, and the noble and deadly dremora. The crocodile-headed humanoid Daedra called the daedroth is a servant of Molag Bal, while the giant but dim-witted ogrim is a servant of Malacath. Sheogorath's lesser Daedra, the golden saint, a half-clothed human female in appearance, is highly resistant to magic and a dangerous spellcaster.

Another type of lesser Daedra often encountered in Morrowind is the Atronach, or Elemental Daedra. Atronachs have no binding kinship or alignments with the Daedra Lords, serving one realm or another at whim, shifting sides according to seduction, compulsion, or opportunity.

Varieties of Daedra

by Aranea Drethan, Healer and Dissident Priest

An analysis of Daedra forms, focusing primarily on the Dremora

There is little chance of our ever understanding the various orders of Daedra and their relationships to the Daedra Lords and their dominions. Of the varieties of Daedra that appear in our world, and the varieties of their relationships to their fellows and their Daedra patrons, there is no end. In one place and time they are seen to be this, and in another place and time they are seen to be the opposite, and in another place and time they are seen to be both this and that, in completely contradictory terms.

What Daedra serves this Prince? What Daedra gives orders, and what Daedra serves, and in what hierarchy, and under what circumstances? What Daedra exist in fellowship with one another, and what Daedra have eternal enmity to one another, and what Daedra are solitary, or social, and by turns solitary or social? There are no limits to the varieties of behaviors that may be observed, and in one place they may be this, and in another place they may that, and all rules describing them are always found to be contradictory and in exception to others.

Further, from whom may we seek answers to our questions about these orders? From mortals, who know little but what they may observe of another world? From the gods, who speak in riddles, of enigmas wrapped in mysteries, and who keep things from us, the better to preserve their dominion over us? From the Daedra themselves, who are never the models of straightforwardness or truthtelling, but rather are famous for misstatements and obfuscations?

And even were the Daedra to speak the truth, how can we know if they know themselves, or that there is any truth about them that is to be known, or are all arrangements among the Daedra protean and ever subject to change?

In short, what is to be known is little, and what is to be trusted is nothing.

These things being said, I shall venture to relate what I have observed and heard of the relationships of the servants of Lord Dagon in my brief service to the Telvanni Wizard Divayth Fyr, when I sought him out and offered to bring peace to the victims of corprus in his sanitarium, once the Prophecies of the Incarnate had been fulfilled, and Dagoth Ur had been destroyed, and the Blight had been banished from the island of Vvardenfell forever.

Divayth Fyr told me that he, by choice, trafficked only with two Daedra Powers — Mehrunes Dagon and Azura.

Azura, he said, knew and understood all things, and declined to speak of these things, or only spoke in riddles.

Mehrunes Dagon, on the other hand, out of pride, fixity of purpose, and a predictable lack of subtlety in thought, knew nothing and understood nothing, and was inclined to speak freely and without falsehood.

Divayth Fyr said that Dagon's chief servants, the Dremora, were like him in pride, fixed purpose, and lack of subtlety, with the addition of the peculiar traits of honor and loyalty, both within their class and within their relationship to Lord Dagon.

And Divayth Fyr said that the Dremora were ordered into clans and castes, and these clans and castes were well-defined. Individual Dremora might rise or fall in ranks, or move back and forth among clans, but only when regulated by complex oaths, and only at the will and pleasure of their Lord Dagon.

The Dremora refer to themselves as 'The Kyn' ('the People'), contrasting themselves to other Daedra, whom they consider unthinking animals. The term 'kynaz' refers to a member of the Dremora race ('he of the Kyn').

The least of kyn castes are the Churls, the undistinguished rabble of the lowest rank of Dremora. Churls are obsequious to superiors but ferociously cruel to humans and other Daedra.

Next in rank are the Caitiffs, creatures of uncalculating zeal, energy without discrimination. Caitiffs are used as irregulars in the faction wars of the Daedra, as berserkers and shock troops, undisciplined and unreliable, but eager and willing.

The highest of the regular rank-and file of Dremora troops are the Kynvals, warrior-knights who have distinguished themselves in battle, and shown the deliberate steadiness of potential war leaders.

Above the rank and file warriors of the Churl, Caitiff, and Kynval castes are the officer castes.

A Kynreeve is a clan sheriff or clan officer. Kynreeves are typically associated either with a clan fighting unit or an administrative office in the order of battle.

The Kynmarcher is the lord and high officer of a Daedric citadel, outpost, or gate. A Kymarcher's command is usually associated both with a unit and with a 'fief — a location or territory for which he is responsible.

Above the Kymarcher is the Markynaz, or 'grand duke'. A Markynaz is a lord of lords, and member of the Markyn, Mehrunes Dagon's Council of Lords.

The highest rank of Dremora is the Valkynaz, or 'prince'. This warrior duke is a member of the Valkyn, Mehrunes Dagon's personal guard. The Valkynaz are rarely encountered on Tamriel; normally they remain by Mehrunes Dagon's side, or serve as commanders of operations of particular importance or interest to Dagon.

Of the varieties of other Daedra I encountered while I served in Divayth Fyr's Corprusarium — Ogrims and Golden Saints, Daedroths and Winged Twilights, Scamps and Clannfear — there is much that might be said, but little that is helpful or reliable.

I did note, however, that when Divayth Fyr sought a Daedra of a character like unto the Dremora, but of greater power, and greater inclination for independence and initiative, or solely as a master, he summoned Xivilai, who are like the Dremora in personality and temperament, except that they hate subordination, and are liable to disloyalty and betrayal when they feel they have not been treated with the proper deference and respect.

The feral, beastlike Daedra like the Clannfear and the Daedroth appear in the service of many different Daedric Powers, and may represent common creatures existing like wild animals in the wildernesses of Oblivion. Other savage, semi-intelligent creatures like Scamps and Spider Daedra may also be found in the realms of various Daedra Lords.

The case of the Elemental Atronachs, on the other hand, is less certain. Flame and Frost Atronachs, for example, appear to be highly intelligent, but not all varieties of Elemental Atronachs seem to be social or to have the power of speech. Divayth Fyr preferred not to summon or deal with these creatures, had little experience with them, and showed no inclination to speculate upon their nature, so I learned little about them during my time at Tel Fyr.

Spirit of the Daedra

A look into the Daedric mindset

HOW YOU SHOULD KNOW US
DEATH, DEFEAT, AND FEAR

We do not die. We do not fear death.

Destroy the Body, and the Animus is cast into The Darkness. But the Animus returns.

But we are not all brave.

We feel pain, and fear it. We feel shame, and fear it. We feel loss, and fear it. We hate the Darkness, and fear it.

The Scamps have small thoughts, and cannot fear greatly.

The Vermai have no thoughts, and cannot fear.

The Dremora have deep thoughts, and must master fear to overcome it.

THE CLAN BOND

We are not born; we have not fathers nor mothers, yet we have kin and clans.

The clan-form is strong. It shapes body and thought.

In the clan-form is strength and purpose.

THE OATH BOND

We serve by choice. We serve the strong, so that their strength might shield us.

Clans serve by long-practice, but practice may change.

Dremora have long served Dagon but not always so.

Practice is secure when oath-bonds are secure, and trust is shared.

When oath-bonds are weak, there is pain, and shame, and loss, and Darkness, and great fear.

HOW WE THINK ABOUT MAN

Perhaps you find Scamps comic, and Vermai brutish.

How then do you imagine we view you humans?

You are the Prey, and we are the Huntsmen.

The Scamps are the Hounds, and the Vermai the Beaters.

Your flesh is sweet, and the chase is diverting.

As you may sometimes praise the fox or hare, admiring its cunning and speed, and lamenting as the hounds tear its flesh, so do we sometimes admire our prey, and secretly applaud when it cheats our snares or eludes pursuit.

But, like all worldly things, you will in time wear, and be used up. You age, grow ugly, weak, and foolish. You are always lost, late or soon.

Sometimes the prey turns upon us and bites. It is a small thing. When wounded or weary, we fly away to restore. Sometimes a precious thing is lost, but that risk makes the chase all the sweeter.

MAN'S MYSTERY
Man is mortal, and doomed to death and failure and loss.
This lies beyond our comprehension — why do you not despair?

Invocation of Azura

by Sigillah Parate

For three hundred years I have been a priestess of Azura, the Daedric Princess of Moonshadow, Mother of the Rose, and Queen of the Night Sky. Every Hogithum, which we celebrate on the 21st of First Seed, we summon her for guidance, as well as to offer things of worth and beauty to Her Majesty. She is a cruel but wise mistress. We do not invoke her on any Hogithum troubled by thunderstorms, for those nights belong to the Mad One, Sheogorath, even if they do coincide with the occasion. Azura at such times understands our caution.

Azura's invocation is a very personal one. I have been priestess to three other Daedric Princes, but Azura values the quality of her worshippers, and the truth behind our adoration of her. When I was a Dark Elven maid of sixteen, I joined my grandmother's coven, worshippers of Molag Bal, the Schemer Princess. Blackmail, extortion, and bribery are as much the weapons of the Witches of Molag Bal as is dark magic. The Invocation of Molag Bal is held on the 20th of Evening Star, except during stormy weather. This ceremony is seldom missed, but Molag Bal often appears to her cultists in mortal guise on other dates. When my grandmother died in an attempt to poison the heir of Firewatch, I re-examined my faith in the cult.

My brother was a wizard of the cult of Boethiah–and from what he told me, the Dark Warrior was closer to my spirit than the treacherous Molag Bal. Boethiah is a Warrior Princess who acts more overtly than any other Daedroth. After years of skulking and scheming, it felt good to perform acts for a mistress which had direct, immediate consequences. Besides, I liked it that Boethiah was a Daedra of the Dark Elves. Our cult would summon her on the day we called the Gauntlet, the 2nd of Sun's Dusk. Bloody competitions would be held in her honor, and the duels and battles would continue until nine cultists were killed at the hands of other cultists. Boethiah cared little for her cultists–she only cared for our blood. I do think I saw her smile when I accidentally slew my brother in a sparring session. My horror, I think, greatly pleased her.

I left the cult soon after that. Boethiah was too impersonal for me, too cold. I wanted a mistress of greater depth. For the next eighteen years of my life, I worshipped no one. Instead I read and researched. It was in an old and profane tome that I came upon the name of Nocturnal–Nocturnal the Night Mistress, Nocturnal the Unfathomable. As the book prescribed, I called to her on her holy day, the 3rd of Hearth Fire. At last I had found the personal mistress I had so long desired. I strove to understand her labyrinthine philosophy, the source of her mysterious pain. Everything about her was dark and shrouded, even the way she spoke and the acts she required of me. It took years for me to understand the simple fact that I could never understand Nocturnal. Her mystery was as essential to her as savagery was to Boethiah or treachery was to

Molag Bal. To understand Nocturnal is to negate her, to pull back the curtains cloaking her realm of darkness. As much as I loved her, I recognized the futility of unraveling her enigmas. I turned instead to her sister, Azura.

Azura is the only Daedra Princess I have ever worshipped who seems to care about her followers. Molag Bal wanted my mind, Boethiah wanted my arms, and Nocturnal perhaps my curiosity. Azura wants all of that, and our love above all. Not our abject slavering, but our honest and genuine caring in all its forms. It is important to her that our emotions be engaged in her worship. And our love must also be directed inward. If we love her and hate ourselves, she feels our pain. I will, for all time, have no other mistress.

Azura and the Box

by Marobar Sul

Part XI

Nchylbar had enjoyed an adventurous youth, but had grown to be a very wise, very old Dwemer who spent his life searching for the truth and dispelling superstitions. He invented much and created many theorems and logic structures that bore his name. But much of the world still puzzled him, and nothing was a greater enigma to him than the nature of the Aedra and Daedra. Over the course of his research, he came to the conclusion that many of the Gods were entirely fabricated by man and mer.

Nothing, however, was a greater question to Nchylbar than the limits of divine power. Were the Greater Beings the masters of the entire world, or did the humbler creatures have the strength to forge their own destinies? As Nchylbar found himself nearing the end of his life, he felt he must understand this last basic truth.

Among the sage's acquaintances was a holy Chimer priest named Athynic. When the priest was visiting Bthalag–Zturamz, Nchylbar told him what he intended to do to find the nature of divine power. Athynic was terrified and pleaded with his friend not to break this great mystery, but Nchylbar was resolute. Finally, the priest agreed to assist out of love for his friend, though he feared the results of this blasphemy.

Athynic summoned Azura. After the usual rituals by which the priest declared his faith in her powers and Azura agreed to do no harm to him, Nchylbar and a dozen of his students entered the summoning chamber, carrying with them a large box.

"As we see you in our land, Azura, you are the Goddess of the Dusk and Dawn and all the mysteries therein," said Nchylbar, trying to appear as kindly and obsequious as he could be. "It is said that your knowledge is absolute."

"So it is," smiled the Daedra.

"You would know, for example, what is in this wooden box," said Nchylbar.

Azura turned to Athynic, her brow furrowed. The priest was quick to explain, "Goddess, this Dwemer is a very wise and respected man. Believe me, please, the intention is not to mock your greatness, but to demonstrate it to this scientist and to the rest of his skeptical race. I have tried to explain your power to him, but his philosophy is such that he must see it demonstrated."

"If I am to demonstrate my might in a way to bring the Dwemer race to understanding, it might have been a more impressive feat you would have me do," growled Azura, and turned to look Nchylbar in the eyes. "There is a red–petalled flower in the box."

Nchylbar did not smile or frown. He simply opened the box and revealed to all that it was empty.

When the students turned to look to Azura, she was gone. Only Athynic had seen the Goddess's expression before she vanished, and he could not speak, he was trembling so. A curse had fallen, he knew that truly, but even crueler was the knowledge of divine power that had been demonstrated. Nchylbar also looked pale, uncertain on his feet, but his face shone with not fear, but bliss. The smile of a Dwemer finding evidence for a truth only suspected.

Two of his students supported him, and two more supported the priest as they left the chamber.

"I have studied very much over the years, performed countless experiments, taught myself a thousand languages, and yet the skill that has taught me the finally truth is the one that I learned when I was but a poor, young man, trying only to have enough gold to eat," whispered the sage.

As he was escorted up the stairs to his bed, a red flower petal fell from the sleeve of his voluminous robe. Nchylbar died that night, a portrait of peace that comes from contented knowledge.

Publisher's Note:

This is another tale whose origin is unmistakably Dwemer. Again, the words of some Aldmeris translations are quite different, but the essence of the story is the same. The Dunmer have a similar tale about Nchylbar, but in the Dunmer version, Azura recognizes the trick and refuses to answer the question. She slays the Dwemer present for their skepticism and curses the Dunmer for blasphemy.

In the Aldmeris versions, Azura is tricked not by an empty box, but by a box containing a sphere which somehow becomes a flat square. Of course the Aldmeris versions, being a few steps closer to the original Dwemer, are much more difficult to understand. Perhaps this "stage magic" explanation was added by Gor Felim because of Felim's own experience with such tricks in his plays when a mage was not available.

"Marobar Sul" left even the character of Nchylbar alone, and he represents many "Dwemer" virtues. His skepticism, while not nearly as absolute as in the Aldmeris version, is celebrated even though it brings a curse upon the Dwemer and the unnamed House of the poor priest.

Whatever the true nature of the Gods, and how right or wrong the Dwemer were about them, this tale might explain why the dwarves vanished from the face of Tamriel. Though Nchylbar and his kind may not have intended to mock the Aedra and Daedra, their skepticism certainly offended the Divine Orders.

The Anticipations

The Daedra are powerful ancestor spirits, similar in form and substance to the Tribunal (Blessed Be Their Holy Names), but weaker in power, and more arbitrary and removed from the affairs of mortals. In old times, the Chimer worshiped the Daedra as gods. But they did not deserve this veneration, for the Daedra harm their worshippers as often as help them.

The Advent of the Tribunal (Blessed Be Their Holy Names) changed this unhappy state. By the Apotheosis, the Tribunal (Blessed Be Their Holy Names) became the Protectors and High Ancestor Spirits of the Dunmer, and bade the Daedra to give proper veneration and obedience. The Three Good Daedra, Boethiah, Azura, and Mephala, recognized the Divinity of the Triune Ancestors (Blessed Be Their Holy Names). The Rebel Daedra, Molag Bal, Malacath, Sheogorath, and Mehrunes Dagon, refused to swear fealty to the Tribunal (Blessed Be Their Holy Names), and their worshippers were cast out.

These Rebel Daedra thus became the Four Corners of the House of Troubles, and they continue to plague our tranquility and tempt the unwary into Heresy and Dark Worship. The Priests of the Temple remain ever vigilant for signs of the Adversaries' return, sometimes aided by the loyal Three Good Daedra, who are familiar with the wiles of their rebellious kin.

The Good Daedra are known to the Temple as the Anticipations, since they are the early ancestral anticipations of the loving patronage of the Tribunal. The Anticipations are the Daedra Lords Boethiah, Mephala, and Azura.

Boethiah is the Anticipation of Almalexia but male to her female. Boethiah was the ancestor who illuminated the elves ages ago before the Mythic Era. He told them the truth of Lorkhan's test, and defeated Auriel's champion, Trinimac. Boethiah ate Trinimac and voided him. The followers of Boethiah and Trinimac rubbed the soil of Trinimac upon themselves and changed their skins.

Mephala is the Anticipation of Vivec, but manifold and androgynous. Mephala taught the Chimer to evade their enemies or kill them with secret murder. Enemies were numerous in those days since the Chimer were a small with enemies on all sides. Mephala organized the clan systems that eventually became the Great Houses. Later, Mephala created the Morag Tong.

Azura is the Anticipation of Sotha Sil, but female to his male. Azura was the ancestor who taught the Chimer how to be different from the Altmer. Her teachings are sometimes attributed to Boethiah. In the stories, Azura is often encountered more as a communal progenitor of the race as a whole rather than as an individual ancestor. She is associated with Dusk and Dawn, and is sometimes called the Mother Soul. Azura's Star, also called the Twilight Star, appears briefly at dawn and dusk low on the horizon below the constellation of the Steed. Azura is associated with mystery and magic, fate and prophecy.

Beggar Prince

The story of Wheedle and his gifts from the Daedric Lord Namira

We look down upon the beggars of the Empire. These lost souls are the poor and wretched of the land. Every city has its beggars. Most are so poor they have only the clothes on their backs. They eat the scraps the rest of us throw out. We toss them a coin so that we don't have to think too long about their plight.

Imagine my surprise when I heard the tale of the Beggar Prince. I could not imagine what a Prince of Beggars would be. Here is the tale I heard. It takes place in the first age, when gods walked like men and daedra stalked the wilderness with impunity. It is a time before they were all confined to Oblivion...

There once was a man named Wheedle. Or maybe it was a woman. The story goes to great lengths to avoid declaring Wheedle's gender. Wheedle was the 13th child of a king in Valenwood. As such Wheedle was in no position to take the throne or even inherit much property or wealth.

Wheedle had left the palace to find independent fortune and glory. After many days of endless forest roads and tiny villages, Wheedle came upon three men surrounding a beggar. The beggar was swaddled in rags from head to toe. No portion of the vagabond's body was visible. The men were intent on slaying the beggar.

With a cry of rage and indignation, Wheedle charged the men with sword drawn. Being simple townsfolk, armed only with pitchforks and scythes, they immediately fled from the armored figure with the shining sword.

"Many thanks for saving me," wheezed the beggar from beneath the heap of foul rags. Wheedle could barely stand the stench.

"What is your name, wretch?" Wheedle asked.

"I am Namira."

Unlike the townsfolk, Wheedle was well learned. That name meant nothing to them, but to Wheedle it was an opportunity.

"You are the Daedric lord!" Wheedle exclaimed. "Why did you allow those men to harass you? You could have slain them all with a whisper."

"I am please you recognized me," Namira rasped. "I am frequently reviled by townsfolk. It pleases me to be recognized for my attribute, if not for my name."

Wheedle knew that Namira was the Daedric lord of all thing gross and repulsive. Diseases such as leprosy and gangrene were her domain. Where others might have seen danger, Wheedle saw opportunity.

"Oh, great Namira, let me apprentice myself to you. I ask only that you grant me powers to make my fortune and forge a name for myself that will live through the ages."

"Nay. I make my way alone in the world. I have no need for an apprentice."

Namira shambled off down the road. Wheedle would not be put off. With a bound, Wheedle was at Namira's heel, pressing the case for an apprenticeship. For 33 days and night, Wheedle kept up the debate. Namira said nothing, but Wheedle's voice was ceaseless. Finally, on the 33rd day, Wheedle was too hoarse to talk.

Namira looked back on the suddenly silent figure. Wheedle knelt in the mud at her feet, open hands raised in supplication.

"It would seem you have completed your apprenticeship to me after all," Namira declared. "I shall grant your request."

Wheedle was overjoyed.

"I grant you the power of disease. You may choose to be afflicted with any disease you choose, changing them at will, so long as it has visible symptoms. However, you must always bear at least one.

"I grant you the power of pity. You may evoke pity in anyone that sees you.

"Finally, I grant you the power of disregard. You may cause others to disregard your presence."

Wheedle was aghast. These were not boons from which a fortune could be made. They were curses, each awful in its own right, but together they were unthinkable.

"How am I to make my fortune and forge a name for myself with these terrible gifts?"

"As you begged at my feet for 33 days and 33 nights, so shall you now beg for your fortune in the cities of men. Your name will become legendary among the beggars of Tamriel. The story of Wheedle, the Prince of Beggars, shall be handed down throughout the generations.

It was as Namira predicted. Wheedle was an irresistible beggar. None could see the wretch without desperately wanting to toss a coin at the huddled form. However, Wheedle also discovered that the power of disregard gave great access to the secrets of the realms. People unknowingly said important things where Wheedle could hear them. Wheedle grew to know the comings and goings of every citizen in the city.

To this day, it is said that if you really want to know something, go ask the beggars. They have eyes and ears throughout the cities. They know all the little secrets of the daily lives of its citizens.

Changed Ones

f all the et'Ada who wandered Nirn, Trinimac was the strongest. He, for a very long time, fooled the Aldmeri into thinking that tears were the best response to the Sundering. They cried and shamed our ancestors, especially the feminine Altmer. They even took the Missing God's name in vain, calling His narratives into question. So one day Boethiah, Prince of Plots, precocious youth, tricked Trinimac to go into his mouth. Boethiah talked like Trinimac for awhile then, and gathered enough people to listen to him. Boethiah showed them the lies of the et'Ada, the Aedra, and told them Trinimac was the biggest liar of all, saying all this with Trinimac's voice! Boethiah told the mass before him the Tri-Angled Truth. He showed them, with Mephala, the rules of Psijic Endeavor. He taught them how to build Houses, and what items they needed to bury in the Corners. He demonstrated the right way to wear their skin. He performed the way to walk to achieve an Exodus. Then Boethiah relieved himself of Trinimac right there on the ground before them to prove all the things he said were the truth. It was easy then for his new people to become the Changed Ones.

Wabbajack

Little boys shouldn't summon up the forces of eternal darkness unless they have an adult supervising, I know, I know. But on that sunny night on the 5th of First Seed, I didn't want an adult. I wanted Hermaeus Mora, the daedra of knowledge, learning, gums, and varnishes. You see, I was told by a beautiful, large breasted man who lived under the library in my home town that the 5th of First Seed was Hermaeus Mora's night. And if I wanted the Oghma Infinium, the book of knowledge, I had to summon him. When you're the new king of Solitude, every bit of knowledge helps.

Normally, you need a witches coven, or a mages guild, or at least matching pillow case and sheets to invoke a prince of Oblivion. The Man Under the Library showed me how to do it myself. He told me to wait until the storm was at its height before shaving the cat. I've forgotten the rest of the ceremony. It doesn't matter.

Someone appeared who I thought was Hermaeus Mora. The only thing that made me somewhat suspicious was Hermaeus Mora, from what I read, was a big blobby multi-eyed clawed monstrosity, and this guy looked like a waistcoated banker. Also, he kept calling himself Sheogorath, not Hermaeus Mora. Still, I was so happy to have successfully summoned Hermaeus Mora, these inconsistencies did not bother me. He had me do some things that didn't make any sense to me (beyond the mortal scope, breadth, and ken, I suppose), and then his servant happily gave me something he called the Wabbajack. Wabbajack. Wabbajack.

Wabbajack.

Wabbajack. Wabbajack. Wabbajack. Wabbajack. Wabbajack. Wabbajack.

Maybe the Wabbajack is the Book of Knowledge. Maybe I'm smarter because I know cats can be bats can be rats can be hats can be gnats can be thats can be thises. And that doors can be boars can be snores can be floors can be roars can be spores can be yours can be mine. I must be smart, for the interconnective system is very clear to me. Then why, or wherefore do people keep calling me mad?

Wabbajack. Wabbajack. Wabbajack.

The Woodcutter's Wife

by Mogen Son of Molag

 story of mistrust, murder, and magic.

Legend tells of a woodcutter who built a shack deep within the pine forest. There, he hoped to live in peace with his family.

The woodcutter's family lived well for a time, but without warning, the weather turned bitterly cold and spoiled the harvest. Before long, with their meager supply of food all but gone, the family was starving.

Late one snowy night, a traveler knocked on the cabin door seeking shelter from the biting cold. Always generous of heart, the woodcutter welcomed the stranger into his home, apologizing that he had no food to offer.

With a smile, the traveler cast off his cloak to reveal the garments of a mage. As the woodcutter and his family looked on, the mysterious visitor reached into his satchel and withdrew a scroll tied with a silver ribbon. No sooner had the wizard unfurled the scroll and read the words aloud, when a great feast appeared from out of thin air. That night, nobody in the woodcutter's cabin went hungry.

Day by day, the snow piled up. Every night, the mage produced another scroll from his bag and read the words, each time summoning a new feast. On the fifth night, the woodcutter's wife awoke her husband to confess her mistrust of their magical guest. Surely, she argued, there was some price to pay for the magical feasts that everyone enjoyed night after night.

The woodcutter would have none of it. After nearly dying from the lack of food, his family was eating well. The divines had sent them a gift, he explained, and it was foolish to question their wisdom.

But the woodcutter's wife would not be persuaded. Every night, she grew more fearful and more desperate. She was certain that the family had entered into a devil's bargain, and the time would soon come when the mage would ask for something unspeakable in return for his gifts.

While everyone in the cabin slept, the woodcutter's wife snuck out of bed and took her husband's axe in hand. She crept into the traveler's room and with one swing, lopped off his head.

Suddenly, the wizard's disembodied head awoke. His eyes opened wide and when he beheld his maimed body, he let forth a terrible cry.

Awakened by the horrified scream, the woodcutter and his children rushed into the room and gasped at the terrible sight of the decapitated mage.

With his last gasp of breath, the traveler laid a fearful curse on the woodcutter's wife. After her mortal death, she was damned to rise once again and walk the woods alone only to burn at the rising of the sun.

To this day, those who walk the pine forest late at night tell tales of a weeping woman glimpsed between the trees. She carries a bloody axe, the stories say, and is terrifying to behold.

The Cabin in the Woods

by Mogen Son of Molag

tale of a soldier and a sobbing ghost.

Late one night a few seasons ago, a soldier was returning home after several bloody battles. He decided he would save some gold and decided to cross the pine forest on foot.

The first day of his journey was rather uneventful, the soldier stuck to the main path and kept a brisk pace. When it started getting dark he setup his bedroll, built a small fire and cooked up some rabbit he had caught. "A fine day indeed" he thought to himself as he fell asleep.

Partway through the evening the soldier was woken up by soft sobbing in the distance. He grabbed his sword assuming it to be a bandit trick, but pretended to sleep so he could get the jump on them. After a few minutes the sobbing started moving away from his camp until he could no longer hear it. For the rest of the night he slept with one eye open.

Day two the soldier awoke from what rotten sleep he could catch and started off through the forest at a quicker pace, intending to put distance between himself and whatever he had heard last night. As the day went on it began to rain heavy so the soldier built himself a little shelter for the evening so he could remain dry while he slept.

It took him a little longer to fall asleep with thoughts of the previous night fresh in his mind but he eventually slept.

This time he awoke to sobbing that sounded like it was right outside his shelter. The soldier grabbed his sword and crawled out of the shelter. In front of the fire he saw the back of a ghostly woman sobbing into her hands.

The soldier mustered his courage and asked her what was wrong.

No answer.

He began to slowly approach but before he could reach her she turned and screamed at him. The ghostly woman raised an axe and began to run at the soldier, disappearing before she made contact.

The soldier took off into the night with just his sword in hand. He ran until the first light of dawn where he started down the road again, as fast as he could move.

The third day was bright and sunny, but the soldier, rattled and sleepless, didn't even notice. He moved as fast as he could trying to get through the forest before nightfall.

As darkness began to fall he saw a cabin just off the road and thought to himself it would be a good place to hunker down for the night. After arriving at the cabin he spent some time blocking the doors and windows, nothing would get in.

Despite his preparations, he could not sleep. He sat in what used to be the cabin's bedroom staring at the barricaded door shaking. Eventually he could keep his eyes open no longer and fell asleep.

This time he awoke to laughing on the other side of the barricaded door. It sounded like the woman from before, but he refused to believe it was her.

The soldier burst through the barricaded door into the main room to find the ghostly woman from the night before staring at the ground laughing hysterically with axe in hand.

He began to relentlessly attack the ghostly woman but he could feel his strikes were less effective. He used a scroll of firebolt which drew a scream from her and she exploded, disappearing.

The ordeal was over, the ghost was gone.

The soldier slept well that night and the next day made excellent distance through the woods. As the sun began to set he came out on the other side of the forest and looked back, remembering the days before.

As he turned and started walking away from the woods he could swear he heard the sobbing again.

The House of Troubles

Among the ancient ancestral spirits who accompanied Saint Veloth and the Chimer into the promised land of Morrowind, the four Daedra Lords, Malacath, Mehrunes Dagon, Molag Bal, and Sheogorath, are known as the Four Corners of the House of Troubles. These Daedra Lords rebelled against the counsel and admonition of the Tribunal, causing great kinstrife and confusion among the clans and Great Houses.

Malacath, Mehrunes Dagon, Molag Bal, and Sheogorath are holy in that they serve the role of obstacles during the Testing. Through time they have sometimes become associated with local enemies, like the Nords, Akaviri, or Mountain Orcs.

Malacath is the reanimated dung that was Trinimac, Malacath is a weak but vengeful god. The Dark Elves say he is Malak, the god-king of the orcs. He tests the Dunmer for physical weakness.

Molag Bal is, in Morrowind, the King of Rape. He tries to upset the bloodlines of Houses and otherwise ruin the Dunmer gene pool. A race of monsters, said to live in Molag Amur, are the result of his seduction of Vivec during the previous era.

Sheogorath is the King of Madness. He always tests the Dunmer for mental weakness. In many legends he is called upon by one Dunmer faction against another; in half of these stories he does not betray those who called him, further confusing the issue of his place in the scheme of things (can he help us? is he not an obstacle?). He is often associated with the fear other races have of the Dunmer, especially those who, like the Empire, might prove as useful allies.

Mehrunes Dagon is the god of destruction. He is associated with natural dangers like fire, earthquakes, and floods. To some he represents the inhospitable land of Morrowind. He tests the Dunmer will to survive and persevere.

The worship of these four malevolent spirits is against the law and practice of the Temple. However, the Four Corners seldom fail to discover those greedy, reckless, or mad enough to serve them. By ancient Temple law and custom, and also by imperial law, the lives of witches and warlocks are forfeit, and Imperial garrisons join Ordinators and Buoyant Armigers of the Temple in tracking down and destroying these foul covens in the wilderness refuges and ancient ruins where they conceal their profane worships.

Opusculus Lamae Bal ta Mezzamortie: A Brief Account of Lamae Bal and the Restless Death

Mabei Aywenil, Scribe

Translation by University of Gwylim Press: 3E 105

As brighter grows light, darker becomes shadow. So it passed that the Daedra Molag Bal looked on Arkay and thought the Aedra prideful of his dominion o'er the death of man and mer, and it was sooth.

Bal, whose sphere is the wanton oppression and entrapment of mortal souls, sought to thwart Arkay, who knew that not man, nor mer, nor beastfolk of all Nirn could escape eventual death. The Aedra was doubtless of his sphere, and so Molag Bal set upon Nirn to best death.

Tamriel was still young, and filled with danger and wondrous magick when Bal walked in the aspect of a man and took a virgin, Lamae Beolfag, from the Nedic Peoples. Savage and loveless, Bal profaned her body, and her screams became the Shrieking Winds, which still haunt certain winding fjords of Skyrim. Shedding a lone droplet of blood on her brow, Bal left Nirn, having sown his wrath.

Violated and comatose, Lamae was found by nomads, and cared for. A fortnight hence, the nomad wyrd-woman enshrouded Lamae in pall for she had passed into death. In their way, the nomads built a bonfire to immolate the husk. That night, Lamae rose from her funeral pyre, and set upon the coven, still aflame. She ripped the throats of the women, ate the eyes of the children, and raped their men as cruelly as Bal had ravished her.

And so; Lamae, (who is known to us as blood-matron) imprecated her foul aspect upon the folk of Tamriel, and begat a brood of countless abominations, from which came the vampires, most cunning of the night-horrors. And so was the scourge of undeath wrought upon Tamriel, cruelly mocking Arkay's rhythm of life and death through all the coming eras of the et'Ada, and for all his sadness, Arkay knew this could not be undone.

Amongst the Draugr

by Bernadette Bantien College of Winterhold

It wasn't until my seventh month with the creatures that they seemed to accept me. Well, "accept" isn't really the proper word, but they seemed to have decided that I posed no threat to them and gradually ceased their attacks. Though more than capable of fending them off (a combination of fire and turning spells are generally sufficient), I admit that I tired of having to be ever vigilant in their presence.

I'll never know whether there was some sort of agreement communicated among them, for the only utterances they make seem to be in that heathen tongue that I can't even pronounce, much less transcribe. In time, I learned more of their intentions towards me from their general movements and tones rather than specific words. Hostility in any creature is easily read, but in these most peculiar of the living dead, with such variations in gait and speed, what amounts to a hostile charge in one may simply be casual movement in another. The eyes seem to be key to their intent, and I will confess to more than one dream haunted by the glowing pinpoints in the darkness.

I had always wondered why the ancient priests of the dragon cult insisted that their followers be buried with them. It seems the height of pagan vanity to drag your conscripts to their death along with you, but as I integrated into their presence, I began to observe the reasons. Every day, a different set of draugr would awaken, shamble their way to the sarcophagus of their priest, and prostrate themselves before it. Several hours of this, followed by a meticulous cleaning of the area. It would appear that the adherents of the dragon priest continue their worship of him in death, which would also explain the ferocity with which they defend his chambers.

It took several weeks before I felt comfortable approaching the dragon priest's resting place, myself. Inch by inch, until the snarling draugrs around me seemed to tire of fending off my timid presence. I was able to set some simple scrying spells around the tomb, that I might get a sense of what magical energies resided there. When the next group of draugr came to pay homage to the priest, I noted a sort of transferal happening. A distinct flow of life force between the adherents and the master.

It was here that I finally understood the dragon cult's notion of resurrection. The second eternal life was only promised to those who ascended to the priesthood, but the lesser functionaries contributed their life force to sustaining them for eternity. I don't know what sort of eternal wellspring they draw from, but it's clear that each draugr carries only the barest whisper of life in it, and rekindles it nightly while resting in its niche. I now believe that the grotesque forms that we see in the barrows were, in fact, buried fully as men and women, and only over the thousands of years that have passed withered into the wretched things we know. If we had visited a barrow directly after its construction, we might not have even known any of its inhabitants were dead!

These discoveries and extrapolations excite me, and my mind aches to return to the barrows. I have only paused here at the College to transcribe these notes and gather further supplies for a more extended stay. My new hope is to learn some rudimentary way of speaking to them, for imagining what they could tell us of the early mists of time is staggering.

Sixteen Accords of Madness

Incomplete accounts of meetings between Sheogorath and the other Daedric Princes

Volume VI

ver proud and boastful, Oblivion's Mad Prince stood one fifth day of mid year among the frigid peaks of Skyrim, and beckoned forth Hircine for parlay. The Huntsman God materialized, for this was his day, and the boldness of Sheogorath intrigued him.

Wry without equal, Sheogorath holds in his realm giggling loons, flamboyant auteurs, and craven mutilators. The Mad Prince will ply profitless bargains and promote senseless bloodshed for nothing more than the joy of another's confusion, tragedy, or rage. So it was that Sheogorath had set a stage on which to play himself as rival to Hircine.

Without haste, the coy Prince proffered his contest; each Prince was to groom a beast to meet at this place again, three years to the hour, and do fatal battle. Expressionless behind his fearsome countenance, Hircine agreed, and with naught but a dusting of snow in the drift, the Princes were gone to their realms.

Confident, but knowing Sheogorath for a trickster, Hircine secretly bred an abomination in his hidden realm. An ancient Daedroth he summoned, and imbued it with the foul curse of lycanthropy. Of pitch heart and jagged fang, the unspeakable horror had no peer, even among the great hunters of Hircine's sphere.

In the third year, on the given day, Hircine returned, where Sheogorath leaned, cross-legged on a stone, whistling with idle patience. The Prince of the Hunt struck his spear to the ground, bringing forth his unnatural, snarling behemoth. Doffing his cap, sly as ever, Sheogorath stood and stepped aside to reveal a tiny, colorful bird perched atop the stone. Demurely it chirped in the bristling gusts, scarcely audible.

In a twisted, springing heap, the Daedroth was upon the stone, leaving only rubble where the boulder had been. Thinking itself victorious, the monster's bloodied maw curled into a mock grin, when a subdued song drifted in the crisp air. The tiny bird lightly hopped along the snout of the furious Daedroth. Sheogorath looked on, quietly mirthful, as the diminutive creature picked at a bit of detritus caught in scales betwixt the fiery eyes of the larger beast. With howling fury, the were-thing blinded itself trying to pluck away the nuisance. And so it continued for hours, Hircine looking on in shame while his finest beast gradually destroyed itself in pursuit of the seemingly oblivious bird, all the while chirping a mournful tune to the lonesome range.

Livid, but beaten, Hircine burned the ragged corpse and withdrew to his realm, swearing in forgotten tongues. His curses still hang in those peaks, and no wayfarer tarries for fear of his wrathful aspect in those obscured heights.

Turning on his heel, Sheogorath beckoned the miniscule songbird to perch atop his shoulder, and strolled down the mountain, making for the warm breezes and vibrant sunsets of the Abecean coast, whistling in tune with the tiniest champion in Tamriel.

Volume IX

Darius Shano found himself running as fast as he could.

He had no idea what he was running from or towards, but he didn't care. The desire saturated his mind — there was nothing in the world except flight. He looked around for landmarks, anything to place himself or to use as a target, but to no avail — the featureless grasslands through which he was sprinting extended as far as the eye could see. "Just have to keep running", he thought to himself. "I have to run as fast as I can". On and on he ran, with no end in sight or in mind....

Standing over Darius Shano while he lay quietly in his bed were his mistress, Vaermina the Dreamweaver, and the Madgod Sheogorath. Vaermina looked down with pride at this disciple of hers, and was boastful of her little jewel.

"Such potential in this one! Through dreams of inspiration, I have nurtured literary talent into fruition, and now he stands in acclaim as an emerging bard and poet! He will gain much favor before I tire of him." Sheogorath, too, gazed at the young Breton artist and saw that he was indeed famous among the other mortals.

"Hmmm," mused Sheogorath, "but how many are there who hate this mortal whom you have built? It is the hatred of the mortals which confirms greatness, and not their love. Surely you can accomplish this as well?"

Vaermina's eyes narrowed. "Yes, the mortals are indeed often foolish and petty, and it is true that many of their most bold have been despised. Do not worry, mad one, for I have the power to achieve many forms of greatness with this one, hatred among them."

"Perhaps, Dreamweaver, it would be amusing to show who has this power? Inspire foolish, arrogant hatred of this mortal for ten years, and then I will do the same. We shall see whose talents are most efficient, free of aid or interference from any of the Daedra."

At this, she relaxed into confident pleasure. "The Madgod is indeed powerful, but this task is suited to my skills. The mortals are repulsed by madness, but rarely think it worthy of hate. I shall take pleasure in revealing this to you, as I bring the more subtle horrors out of this mortal's subconscious."

And so, in the 19th year of his life, the dreams Darius Shano had been experiencing began to change. Fear had always been part of the night for him, but now there was something else. A darkness began to creep into his slumber, a darkness that sucked away all feeling and color, leaving only emptiness behind. When this happened, he opened his mouth to scream, but found that the darkness had taken his voice as well. All he had was the terror and the void, and each night they filled him with a new understanding of death. Yet, when he woke, there was no fear, for he had faith that his Lady had a purpose.

Indeed, one night Vaermina herself emerged from the void. She leaned in close to whisper into his ear.

"Watch carefully, my beloved!" With that, she pulled the void away, and for hours

each night she would reveal to Darius the most horrible perversions of nature. Men being skinned and eaten alive by other men, unimaginable beasts of many limbs and mouths, entire populations being burned –– their screams filled his every evening. In time, these visions gnawed at his soul, and his work began to take on the character of his nightmares. The images revealed to him at night were reproduced on the page, and the terrible cruelty and hollow vice that his work contained both revolted and fascinated the public. They reveled in their disgust over every detail. There were those who openly enjoyed his shocking material, and his popularity among some only fed the hatred of those who found him abhorrent. This continued for several years, while the infamy of Darius grew steadily. Then, in his 29th year, without warning, the dreams and nightmares ceased.

Darius felt a weight lifted, as he no longer endured the nightly tortures, but was confused. "What have I done to displease my Mistress?", he wondered aloud. "Why has she abandoned me?" Vaermina never answered his prayers. No one ever answered, and the restless dreams faded away to leave Darius in long, deep sleeps.

Interest in the works of Darius Shano waned. His prose became stale and his ideas failed to provoke the shock and outrage they once had. As the memory of his notoriety

and of his terrible dreams faded, the questions that raced in his mind eventually produced resentment against Vaermina, his former mistress. Resentment grew into hatred, from hatred came ridicule, and over time ridicule became disbelief. Slowly it became obvious — Vaermina had never spoken to him at all; his dreams were simply the product of a sick mind that had righted itself. He had been deceived by his own subconscious, and the anger and shame overwhelmed him. The man who once conversed with a deity drifted steadily into heresy.

In time, all of the bitterness, doubt, and sacrilege focused in Darius a creative philosophy that was threaded throughout all of his subsequent work. He challenged the Gods themselves, as well as the infantile public and corrupt state for worshipping them. He mocked them all with perverse caricatures, sparing no one and giving no quarter. He challenged the Gods in public to strike him down if they existed, and ridiculed them when no such comeuppance was delivered. To all of this, the people reacted with outrage far greater than they had shown his previous work. His early career had offended only sensibilities, but now he was striking directly at the heart of the people.

His body of work grew in size and intensity. Temples, nobles, and commoners were all targets of his scorn. Finally, at age 39, Darius wrote a piece entitled "The Noblest Fool," ridiculing The Emperor God Tiber Septim for integrating into the pathetic Nine Divines cult. The local King of Daenia, who had been humiliated by this upstart in the past, saw his chance — for his sacrilege against the Empire, Darius Shano was executed, with a ceremonial blade, in front of a cheering crowd of hundreds. His last, bitter words were gurgled through a mouthful of his own blood.

20 years after their wager was first placed, Vaermina and Sheogorath met over Darius Shano's headless corpse. The Dreamweaver had been eager for this meeting; she had been waiting for years to confront the Daedric Prince over his lack of action.

"I have been deceived by you, Sheogorath! I performed my half of the bargain, but during your ten years you never contacted the mortal once. He owes none of his greatness to you or your talents or your influence!"

"Nonsense," croaked the Madgod. "I was with him all along! When your time ended and mine began, your whispers in his ear were replaced with silence. I severed his link to that from which he found the most comfort and meaning, and withheld the very attention the creature so desperately craved. Without his mistress, this man's character could ripen under resentment and hatred. Now his bitterness is total and, overcome by a madness fueled by his rage, he feeds me in my realm as an eternal servant."

Sheogorath turned and spoke to the empty space by his side.

"Indeed; Darius Shano was a glorious mortal. Despised by his own people, his kings, and even by the Gods he mocked. For my success, I shall accept three-score followers of Vaermina into my service. And the dreamers will awaken as madmen."

And thus did Sheogorath teach Vaermina that without madness, there are no dreams, and no creation. Vaermina will never forget this lesson.

Volume XII

In the days before the Orsinium's founding, the spurned Orc-folk were subjected to ostracism and persecutions even more numerous and harsh than their progeny are accustomed to in our own age. So it was that many champions of the Orsimer traveled, enforcing what borders they could for the proliferation of their own people. Many of these champions are spoken of yet today, among them the Cursed Legion, Gromma the Hairless, and the noble Emmeg Gro-Kayra. This latter crusader would have certainly risen to legendary status throughout Tamriel, had he not been subject to the attention of certain Daedric Princes.

Emmeg Gro-Kayra was the bastard son of a young maiden who was killed in childbirth. He was raised by the shaman of his tribe, the Grilikamaug in the peaks of what we now call Normar Heights. Late in his fifteenth year, Emmeg forged by hand an ornate suit of scaled armor, a rite of ascension among his tribe. On a blustery day, he pounded the final rivet, and draping a heavy cloak over the bulky mantle, Emmeg set out from his village for the last time. Word of his exploits always returned home, whether defending merchant caravans from brigands or liberating enslaved beast folk. News of the noble Orc crusader began to grace even the lips of Bretons, often with a tinge of fear.

Less than two years after ascending to maturity, Gro-Kayra was making camp when a thin voice called out from the thickening night. He was surprised to hear the language of his people spoken by a tongue that obviously did not belong to an Orc.

'Lord Kayra', said the voice, 'tales of your deeds have crossed the lips of many, and have reached my ears.' Peering into the murk, Emmeg made out the silhouette of a cloaked figure, made wavy and ephemeral by the hazy campfire. From the voice alone he had thought the interloper an old hag, but he now decided that he was in the presence of a man of slight and lanky build, though he could discern no further detail.

'Perhaps,' the wary Orc began, 'but I seek no glory. Who are you?'

Ignoring the question, the stranger continued, 'Despite that, Orsimer, glory finds you, and I bear a gift worthy of it.' The visitor's cloak parted slightly, revealing nothing but faintly glinting buttons in the pale moonlight, and a bundle was withdrawn and tossed to the side of the fire between the two. Emmeg cautiously removed the rags in which the object was swathed, and was dazzled to discover the item to be a wide, curved blade with ornately decorated handle. The weapon had heft, and Emmeg realized on brandishing it that the elaborate pommel disguised the more practical purpose of balancing the considerable weight of the blade itself. It was nothing much to look at in its present condition, thought the Orc, but once the tarnish was cleaned away and a few missing jewels restored, it would indeed be a blade worthy of a champion ten times his own worth.

'Her name is Neb-Crescen' spoke the thin stranger, seeing the appreciation lighting

Gro–Kayra's face. 'I got her for a horse and a secret in warmer climes, but in my old age I'd be lucky to even lift such a weapon. It's only proper that I pass her on to one such as yourself. To possess her is to change your life, forever.' Overcoming his initial infatuation with the arc of honed steel, Emmeg turned his attention back to the visitor.

'Your words are fine, old man,' Emmeg said, not masking his suspicion, 'but I'm no fool. You traded for this blade once, and you'll trade for it again tonight. What is it that you want?' The stranger's shoulders slumped, and Emmeg was glad to have unveiled the true purpose of this twilight visit. He sat with him a while, eventually offering a stack of furs, warm food, and a handful of coins in exchange for the exotic weapon. By morning, the stranger was gone.

In the week following Emmeg's encounter with the stranger, Neb-Crescen had not left its scabbard. He had encountered no enemy in the woods, and his meals consisted of fowl and small game caught with bow and arrow. The peace suited him fine, but on the seventh morning, while fog still crept between the low-hanging boughs, Emmeg's ears pricked up at the telltale crunch of a nearby footfall in the dense snow and forest debris.

Emmeg's nostrils flared, but he was upwind. Being unable to see or smell his guest, and knowing that the breeze carried his scent in that direction, Emmeg's guard was up, and he cautiously drew Neb-Crescen from its sheath. Emmeg himself was not entirely sure of all that happened next.

The first moment of conscious memory in Emmeg Gro-Kayra's mind after drawing Neb-Crescen was the image of the curved blade sweeping through the air in front of him, spattering blood over the virginal powder coating the forest floor. The second memory was a feeling of frenzied bloodlust creeping over him, but it was then that he saw for the first time his victim, an Orc woman perhaps a few years younger than himself, her body a canvas of grisly wounds, enough to kill a strong man ten times over.

Emmeg's disgust overwhelmed the madness that had overtaken him, and with all his will enlisted, he released Neb-Crescen from his grip and let the blade sail. With a discordant ringing it spun through the air and was buried in a snowdrift. Emmeg fled the scene in shame and horror, drawing the hood of his cloak up to hide himself from the judging eyes of the rising sun.

The scene where Emmeg Gro-Kayra had murdered one of his own kind was a macabre one. Below the neck, the body was flayed and mutilated almost beyond recognition, but the untouched face was frozen in a permanent expression of abject terror.

It was here that Sheogorath performed certain rites that summoned Malacath, and the two Daedric Lords held court in the presence of the disfigured corpse.

'Why show me this, Mad One?' began Malacath, once he recovered from his initial, wordless outrage. 'Do you take such pleasure in watching me grieve the murder of my children?' His guttural voice rumbled, and the patron of the Orsimer looked upon his counterpart with accusing eyes.

'By birth, she was yours, brother outcast,' began Sheogorath, solemn in aspect and demeanor. 'But she was a daughter of mine by her own habits. My mourning here is no less than your own, my outrage no less great.'

'I am not so sure,' grumbled Malacath, 'but rest assured that vengeance for this crime is mine to reap. I expect no contest from you. Stand aside.' As the fearsome Prince began to push past him, Lord Sheogorath spoke again.

'I have no intention of standing between you and vengeance. In fact, I mean to help you. I have servants in this wilderness, and can tell you just where to find our mutual foe. I ask only that you use a weapon of my choosing. Wound the criminal with my blade, and banish him to my plane, where I can exact my own punishment. The rights of honor-killing here belong to you.'

With that, Malacath agreed, took the wide blade from Sheogorath, and was gone.

Malacath materialized in the path of the murderer, the cloaked figure obscured through a blizzard haze. Bellowing a curse so foul as to wilt the surrounding trees, the blade was drawn and Malacath crossed the distance more quickly than a wild fox. Frothing with rage, he swung the blade in a smooth arc which lopped the head of his foe cleanly off, then plunged the blade up to its hilt in his chest, choking off the spurts of blood into a steady, growing stain of red bubbling from beneath the scaled armor and heavy cloak.

Panting from the unexpected immediacy and fury of his own kill, Malacath rested on a knee as the body before him collapsed heavily backwards and the head landed roughly upon a broad, flat stone. The next sound broke the silence like a bolt.

'I — I'm sorry...' sputtered the voice of Emmeg Gro-Kayra. Malacath's eyes went wide as he looked upon the severed head, seeping blood from its wound, but somehow kept alive. Its eyes wavered about wildly, trying to focus on the aspect of Malacath before it. The once-proud eyes of the champion were choked with tears of grief, pain, and confused recognition.

To his horror, Malacath recognized only now that the man he had killed was not only one of his Orsimer children, but very literally a son he had blessed an Orc maiden with years hence. For achingly long moments the two looked upon each other, despondent and shocked.

Then, silent as oiled steel, Sheogorath strode into the clearing. He hefted Emmeg Gro-Kayra's disembodied head and bundled it into a small, grey sack. Sheogorath reclaimed Neb-Crescen from the corpse and turned to walk away. Malacath began to stand, but kneeled again, knowing he had irreversibly damned his own offspring to the realm of Sheogorath, and mourned his failure as the sound of his son's hoarse pleas faded into the frozen horizon.